Observed Dream Movement

Observed Dream Movement

J. Munro Jr.

Columbus, Ohio

This book is a work of fiction. The names, characters and events in this book are the products of the author's imagination or are used fictitiously. Any similarity to real persons living or dead is coincidental and not intended by the author.

The views and opinions expressed in this book are solely those of the author and do not reflect the views or opinions of Gatekeeper Press. Gatekeeper Press is not to be held responsible for and expressly disclaims responsibility of the content herein.

Observed Dream Movement: Zone

Published by Gatekeeper Press
2167 Stringtown Rd, Suite 109
Columbus, OH 43123-2989
www.GatekeeperPress.com

Copyright © 2021 by J. Munro Jr.
All rights reserved. Neither this book, nor any parts within it may be sold or reproduced in any form or by any electronic or mechanical means, including information storage and retrieval systems, without permission in writing from the author. The only exception is by a reviewer, who may quote short excerpts in a review.

Library of Congress Control Number: 2021943334

ISBN (hardcover): 9781662906367
ISBN (paperback): 9781662906374
eISBN: 9781662906381

DEDICATION

In the spirit of Buddhist teachings aligned with the pursuit of social equality it is my deepest wish that all beings become liberated from struggle and suffering. That this wish to find lasting contentment, peace, and joy flourishes. That all of us find the ways and means to attain these states of equilibrium and mental stability. That all people in this great country called the U.S.A., as well as in the rest of the world, strive to increase their innate qualities of patience and understanding. That one day a glorious flag of Earth will fly symbolizing our compassion and inner strength. That we will be inspired by looking at or contemplating this new flag of Earth. That this inspiration will become self-sustaining and will strengthen our motivation to help all others in their pursuit of equanimity, knowledge and wisdom.

ACKNOWLEDGMENTS

With the deepest appreciation, gratitude and love I thank my family.

They have helped me in more ways than I can express. I cannot thank enough current and remote friends and acquaintances who each in their own way have helped me grow both intellectually and spiritually. Without the inspiration and support from all these wonderful people I would not have been able to achieve anything of worth in this world of trial and tribulation. I will never be able to repay their generosity and endless kindness. I do not take credit, or blame, for one concept, thought or word. Everything I have presented in this collection has been said in different ways many times by many people throughout history and prehistory. And it goes without saying by those who possess much more ability and skill in expressing their ideas and knowledge than I. I stand humbled and with great admiration for the multitude of beings who have suffered, worked, studied, and taught. For all those teachers, writers, and people of knowledge in the various disciplines of academics. Those religious disciples and spiritual scholars who have contributed to the plethora of information that we now have at our fingertips. Because of their dedication I have been afforded the great opportunity to at least understand how vast the universe of potential is. How very little I know. I am grateful to have been born in this time and place. For all who have afforded me the resources to live in comfort. For those who have fought, suffered, and died for the ideals of democracy and social equality FOR ALL. Those who died fighting against the Confederacy, Nazis; the Republicans.

They have given us the freedom to pursue our whims of fancy and thought. The historic 2016 reawakening of fascism culminating with the 2021 killing at the White House by the Repubs made me realize how truly lucky I have been. In one way I do thank the Trump-pets. I now realize how many people support unscrupulous liars and their 20,000+ lies. Every day I am grateful that I do not work in one of Trump's sweatshops. At least not yet.

Thank you to all involved with the Oxford Dictionary and Thesaurus. I am a vocabulary indigent. Thank-you Gatekeeper Press. They provide a unique platform enabling people like me to have our thoughts published regardless of literary talent (of course I believe they do have limits). Thanks to Kelly and Dawn for sharing their creative insights. Thank you, Kelly for being a great Author Manager. She guided me through the publishing process with kindness and skill. Thank you to the artists at GKP for their great visual contributions. With highest regards I recommend Gatekeeper Press.

TABLE OF CONTENTS

Acknowledgments	vii
CHAPTER ONE	
A Scottish Descendant	3
Boy in Pew with Mother	5
Suppressed Feelings	7
High Strung	8
Jolt	10
Concussion	11
The Masterpiece Dwelling	12
Profound Question	13
Spring Vacation	14
Passed Out In The Kitchen	16
Winter Debate in a Canadian Tavern I	18
Winter Debate in a Canadian Tavern II	20
A Winters Day in a Suburb of Sub-Zero	23
The Meandering Cat	24
Back Then	25
Haunted Ship	26
A Fireplace Moment	27
CHAPTER TWO	
Observed Dream Movement	31
Mystic Eyes	33

Her Kiss	35
Possessed	36
Sustained Vertex	38
Hopelessly Suspended	39
Lakeside Morning	40
Illuminated Alley	42
Moonlight Trucker	43
Moonlight Hitchhiker	45
Christmas morning Reflection	47
Basis of My Reality	48
Observed- MLK'S Dream Movement	50

CHAPTER THREE

Heretic Wind	55
The Orthodox Nest	57
Crusade	59
The Inquisition	61
In Hypocrites Domain	63
The Crazy Republican Scalpel	65
Lake Lawyer Suicide	66
Philosophy I	68
Philosophy II	70
Mute Spiders Teach Health Care	72
Buddhist/Existential Dichotomy	74
Reunion of Menagerie	75
E.R.	77

Full Code	79
Suchness	81
Somewhere	82
Psychic Vision	83
Unity	85
Himalayan Starlight	87
Simple Thought	89

CHAPTER FOUR

River Death	113
Arctic Hunger	147
A Winter's Nightmare	148
Melting Prism	149
River Insanity	150
Indigenous Rapture	151
After the Apocalypse	152
Asystolic Journey	154
Pre-Historic Flight	156
About the Author	159

CHAPTER ONE

Of Genealogy, Childhood Development
Pre-Grad Education and Young Adult Mania

Observed Dream Movement: Zone

A SCOTTISH DESCENDANT

Highland shadows tell of forefathers hell
                Tree of ingenuity spreading it's germ
Wind from kilts fallen their folklore will be
Their blood and name in honor-
                Passed on to me,

His ancestors bled mountain Foulis
Plaid crests decayed in cold dreary bog
Braveheart warriors through Isle In The Sky they roam
These fearless highland shadows
                Protect descendants home,

From Celtic grounds their souls resound
Ancestral clan Dread-God Immortal
Bagpipes Gaelic in praise of Scottish birth
Proud his noble heritage
Stoic castle
                Crown of firth,

Highland shadows of forefathers tell
Tree of ingenuity spreading it's germ
With his final breath-
Then pure heart freed
His blood and name in honor-
>Passed on to me.

Dedicated to my father, Dr. James Stewart Munro(PhD), who with unwavering determination and diligence worked to overcome the adversities of a broken childhood. Who as an imperfect being dedicated his life to learning, teaching, and supporting his family in better ways than what he knew.

Observed Dream Movement: Zone

BOY IN PEW WITH MOTHER

Church bells glorified Sunday morning game
Arched between stained glass baselines
High fly saints inspired play,
The Alter Boy in batter's box, whiffed the Sermon
Pitch, infield worshipers in pew
Praised God with home run sway,

Vendors walked the isle professing their belief
The soprano sang hymns
From the bleachers for relief
Behind holy plate the priest knew what to say,
The choir stood on deck
I then knelt down to pray;

Please O' Lord , hear my prayer,
Help my Tigers beat theTwins
Please bless my entire family
Protect us from foul ball sins,

Please O' Lord I beg of you
Keep me safe in the strike out zone
Don't let me choke on the host from communion
Let me triple the offering thrown,

Please O' Lord just one more thing
Don't give pick off sign of the cross to Mother
Bless me when I genuflect
Help me sneak home without little brother.

This poem is based on wonderful memories with Patrica Grace Cuddy-Munro, my mother. She has dedicated her life to her faith and to her family without compromise. She is one of the most strong willed and open minded people I have ever known. Without complaint, with the motivation of a tireless saint she dressed, prepared and took five unruly young children to church EVERY SUNDAY. Until we reached the age of rebellion. Which she understood. At the age of 90 she still goes to church EVERY SUNDAY.

SUPPRESSED FEELINGS

Insanity ultimately resonates
                Translucent normalcy
detached
Umbilical cord unraveling, suddenly cordless
Oh thank God we are all attached,

Convulsing pretenders disrupt sleep
Morning ejaculation perpetuates
Self loathing
Rushing emotions-my spineless predator undulates,

Subconscious toxins ferment
Slowly drowning eyes overwhelmed by Truth
Impurities poisonous from ectopic
Childhood
Melancholy cultivates the obtuse vigil.

J. Munro Jr.

HIGH STRUNG

As an unrelenting deluge
        My consciousness expands
From the depths of my spine
Screaming expletives command,

Past the restraints of relativity
Through the icy straits of time
To an incomprehensible plane
Elusive like the perfect crime,

I approach the impending cataclysm
Lonely hearts flutter
The wheel of Karma turns
Brash transmissions sputter,

Under crescent dusk
Half moon shining
Shadow and mist theater
My sanity unwinding,

Observed Dream Movement: Zone

Insecure uncontrolled reveille
        Paralyzing mental congestion
High strung gear wheel machinery working
The sound of silence-clandestine.

J. Munro Jr.

JOLT

Throat sloughing tectonic seizure
    Seismic vulgarity across
      Hemispheres   Neuro-tsunamis
    Reach nirvana
                Cataclysmic signals ignite once calm
       Suppressed raw paranoia
                    Irradiating madness

                Non reflective space

        Warped

Lost time

    Black-whole

CONCUSSION

A dazed vessel leaves tentacles
Galvanized deep unconscious glare
Loose filaments penetrate unexposed clusters
Of the lunatic virus
Endorphins beware,

Ferocious
Faceless
Confused

Yesterday parched in gray matter circus
Voices muddled like Mad Hatter spin
Calliopes awaken the latitude of uncouth Overlord,
The empire of grand swirling hysterics.

J. Munro Jr.

THE MASTERPIECE DWELLING

Impressionists magnum opus depicts necrophiliac amour
Pale copulation with cold porcelain cracks
Cocaine comedy a Cubist's tragic display
Drag queens mimic "The Black Swan Ballet",

Burlesque figurines en vogue improvisation
Baroque envy favors museum décor
Gold diggers rehearse in opera-like brothels
Sculptured faces of idolatry aged-like erosion,

Standing on beliefs entombed like fossils
Medieval lyres dampen musical rings of smoke,
In literary winds volcanic podiums reverberate
In plumes of mythology ruined Athenians choke,

Rome's sprawling legend, a stone mural crumbling
Golden Hieroglyphs stitch the here to Hereafter
Bizarre innuendo inspires uninhibited art
Walnut ruffles strewn across backyard genre
Metaphor incognito-perfect

Anomaly from creation-
Within

Observed Dream Movement: Zone

PROFOUND QUESTION

Idea's travel unknown miles
Contradiction surveys cognitive halls,
Hypotheses create cerebral deviation
Kinetic energy connects subdural walls,

Adrift pondering nature unsolved equation
Arctic deltas question integral reserve
From colder infinity broadband enigmas predominate
Intricate theories anticipate

Hoping answers irrefutably articulate-
The profound.

SPRING VACATION

Dreams and schemes kaleidoscope of sound
Musical notes trickling down
From the mouth of the flutists metallic river
Above sprouting marquee below indigo plateau
Winter's melting trails beckon
Crude Sun God jesters cajole
The glorious spring migration like wildebeest of the Serengeti,
No how bout-like once upon a time:

The Daytona Beach rhapsody a grand chaotic splendor
Melodic wind chimes
Psychedelic folk rhymes
Listening to willow wisps as they gently pass through,

Through looking glass portals white rabbits leap
Melting clock journey like Wonderland sleep
Mescaline skies flattering petals of rain
Never in Never-Never Land springtime mundane,

Observed Dream Movement: Zone

Sparkling humor showering wood-nymph pastel
Into their mouths erotic embers
Margarita's creation a neuro-chemical glance
This marvelous ensemble a tropical Mandala,

My mind an oasis during spring vacation
The Floridian queen's uninhibited dance
Like fluid she flows her eyes the sea,

    I drift

            I drift endlessly

                      La de de la de da

            I drift

And drift……………………………

J. Munro Jr.

PASSED OUT IN THE KITCHEN

Oven light creating cranial formations
Inducing textures
Renouncing late night party scene;
The levee of intoxication bursting
Saxophone sultan belching
Gourmet contents splashing the screen,

No need for particular modes of comfort
No need for a bed or a chair
A wallowing mass   The drunken sea
This overindulgence a cesspool breach for me,

Peaking through cupboards of dire reality
On the cold floor embarrassed and whining
Feelings change as the dishwasher cycles,
Body numb and soft crotch grinding,

Bloodshot eyes like uncooked meat
Lower lip a pendulum of drool
Sagging adipose dragging grout
Peripheral satellites spinning,

Observed Dream Movement: Zone

Fixtures blurred above counter top sink
Garbage can leftovers releasing their stink
With movement ceasing except for a throb
Glowing clock still ticking
A man stumbling across the face of the Earth,

Passed out in the kitchen.

WINTER DEBATE IN A CANADIAN TAVERN I

Ya man I hear you,
You from below the 7th parallel from Santa's reign
Say it does not get cold in southeast Michigan, Ha,
I tell you in temperate laands far wrest of the Prime
Meridon, Where water ice-age archifacs hail a bar tree stands alone.
Iclicles wrangle from it's wibs like Christmas
Ormaments
Shivering in prishtine ishonation. Magfinecient
electromaganets
emit stellar oshcillations across the night sky like
Northern
Lightvectors emblellishing the fridig wind shwpt
valleys of
Eurhopa.
In the cold distance the howl of bluseereeous cosmic
wolves can be heard rahvazging across the forsaken
meeshagainium tundra-eh,
    Hey how about that-eeeh

Observed Dream Movement: Zone

Hey bartender I tthinck I need another drink-eh
Can we pleeze have another round-ehc
    Pleeaze,   eh

Oh by the way is there a wrestoum
In the Canawdioan tavern?

    Is it heated? Ehhhh man

BARTENDER; Ya man, go out the back door
    and turn right-walk past three piles of
    flying reindeer dung-turn left-keep
    going until you stumble past the
    North Pole where you will find it
    on the night before Christmas
    behind the 4th igloo beyond the Polar
    Bear Express-eh,
                    Hey by the way,
Watch out for stampeding Grinch! Eh

Eh-hole.

WINTER DEBATE IN A CANADIAN TAVERN II
(Translation)

Ya man I hear you,
You from below the 7th parallel from Santa's reign
Say it does not get cold in Southeast Michigan.
However, I'll bet that you know that this is true. So please listen
         Carefully. In temperate lands far west of the
         Prime Meridian, where
Watery Ice-age archives hail, a bare tree stands alone. Icicles dangle
From it's limbs like Christmas ornaments shimmering in pristine
Isolation. Across the night sky electromagnetic emissions oscillate Like Northern Light Vectors. Or like stargate fireworks embellishing the Wind-swept valley of Europa. If you are able, if you are not too sloshed
To listen with imagination, in the cold distance the blusterous howl of
Cosmic wolves can be heard as they ravage. As they consume

Observed Dream Movement: Zone

Southeastern Michigan's forsaken snow-covered
tundra-eh. So hey my
Canadian friend-What do you think about that, I think you owe me a
Beer-eh, what do you think about that story-eh.

How about that-eh,

Hey bartender can you get me another
Drink-eh, can we please have another
Round-eh
         Please,

Oh by the way, is there a
Restroom In this Canadian
Tavern?

     Is it heated? Ehhh

BARTENDER; No man, go out the back door-
       Turn right-walk past three piles of flying
       Reindeer dung-turn left- keep going until
       You stumble past the North Pole
       Where you will find it on the night before
       Christmas behind the 4th igloo beyond the

Polar Bear Express-eh
Hey by the way,
      Watch out for stampeding Grinch!
Eh-hole.

Observed Dream Movement: Zone

A WINTERS DAY IN A SUBURB OF SUB-ZERO

It's ten degrees above zero
Some say that is not cold compared to polar
vortex
But there is a bare tree shivering
Shattering the frosted stained glass sky
Solar particles dangling from it's snow covered limbs
A cryogenic embryo in vivo in howling wind,
A cosmic church on a winter's day.

J. Munro Jr.

THE MEANDERING CAT

Meandering cat,

Curiosity tracing lines,
Instincts following design,

Sitting on the porch
Empty barrels behave as chairs
Sun drenched awnings
Creaking stairs,
The call of the wild gusting
Invisible footprints crossin the lawn
Into the neighborhood jungle without a trace
The meandering cat.

The meandering cat-gone.

BACK THEN

Back then I sat in a dark room listening

To the music of Morrison and contemplating
Van Gogh.
Now sitting in a darkroom contemplating
I watch the tree of understanding grow;
I see now back then in darkness I was not
In the vestibule of Enlightenment I sat like a child
Of all that I learned and all that I thought
Because I habitually grasp for desire, I soon forgot.

J. Munro Jr.

HAUNTED SHIP

I sailed away to another shore Far from the dreams
I once beheld
Close to my heart,
Lament
The ravaged beast no longer hunts,
Having forsaken intuition and knowledge
I journey this life

        Like a haunted ship
        Endlessly wandering,

Lost
Alone
Forever in search of elusive forgiveness.

Observed Dream Movement: Zone

A FIREPLACE MOMENT

WASTING HOURS   WASTED FLOWERS

WASTED FLAME   WASTED NAME

                      I think I need to go to sleep now

CHAPTER TWO

Bits and pieces taken from the
Melodramatic garden of idealism
Obsession, passion, self pity and
Other hormone induced behavior

OBSERVED DREAM MOVEMENT

    Awoken from dream I observed your transcendence
Outside deja-vu window premonitions seemed near
During spellbound gaze from third luminosity
    Your suppressed inner beauty suddenly
Suddenly so clear,

Your spirit soaring like surreal bliss
Your destination profound
Astral travel through dreamscape enchanting
Zodiac magic whirling around,

In crystal voidness garland eclipse
Your illusory body like full moon sight
Like bewildering ethereal brilliance
Bellowing passionate shadow bright,

Your eyes a swirling predawn flame
Your flesh a gypsy's twilight see
Deep primitive sorceress
Vast clairvoyant tapestry,

Lucid your movement siren mosaic Earthbound
mistress in euphoria flight
Stardust portrait supernatural projection
Your spectral essence bewitching-

Draped by cumulus night.

MYSTIC EYES

As I try to look past them
Up to the clock
In a cool sultry meadow I wander;
Daydream,

I dream I am lost
In time without cost
Deep mystic eyes
Stars and blue skies,

Can't remember the beginning
The end never a thought
A quiet peaceful rhythm
Voices from those who don't talk,

I sit or I stand, it really does not matter
Neurosis nor mass, inhibit or shatter,

In silence I breathe
This moment without fear
One breath a minute
Could be a light year,

J. Munro Jr.

Her celestial ether I slowly inhale
Upon the cusp of dreams
My lungs like sails,
In the wake of coven mystery
A wavy trance-like sea
Her mystic eyes paradise-

As life can never be.

HER KISS

Her perfectly textured lips
A celestial tapestry designed by Fate
       Like natural overtures-
Immaculate,

Sunrise resurrection illuminates this Earth

Meaningless days dissolve

White horizon oiled with flesh

Subliminal helplessness

Exquisite

To taste from her dripping soul.

J. Munro Jr.

POSSESSED

Possessed, the power of your marrow
 Sending my demons to their depths,
I am in awe of the power of your presence,

Come, enter my epistemic playground
Together we will drink from the chalice of Gnostics,
We will seek extraterrestrial Magi,
Then surrender,

We will laugh at the orthodox faithful
I will refresh your spirit with the intoxicant rebirth
Share with me your moments of death-
I will pool upon the shores of your deathless appendage,

Please, allow me to soothe your habitual narrative,
Lay here with novel intent, perfectly still,
Sighs of temptation unfulfilled My breath alone deep caress
A stranger in your bone temple-obsess,

Observed Dream Movement: Zone

I am freedom eternal-express your unlimited compassion
With each finger explore my hand possessed;
Feel my spirit move
Drift with my passionless thought
Devour my strength
Ascend think not;

Like a cool summer morning awaiting the sun,
I will patiently await your return,

I have tasted your body, I have touched your soul
I now want your deafening silent fear-

POSSESSED!

SUSTAINED VERTEX

Tempo vertex crescendo organic
Your torso pulsating with pelvic rhyme
The sensual tide rising tropical emotion
Each vertebrae touched during passionate
Climb,

A vessel immersed with temporal Indifference,
I arise as maestro reborn
From Atlantis
Your body a melody, a concerto of beauty
Slowly your beauty circulates divine
In oblivion rippling like a mandolin current
Supple cords soothing subterranean sublime,

Listening to symphony of shoreline step
Island castaways harmonic sign
Butterflies coalesce like staccato in droplets
Like the sacred promise to a silent monk
How dark matter orchestrates-
The primitive harbor
How my hypnotic penetration-
Sustains our climax.

Observed Dream Movement: Zone

HOPELESSLY SUSPENDED

Tracing her body through corridors of time
Her lips ritual enigmas mysterious like sphinx
Her mouth Egyptian promising after life pleasure
Her tongue forbidden-
Like cursed pyramid treasure,

Her pupils cankerous alluring Pharaoh
Eyes immortal in Valley of Kings
Goddess of Nile beautiful and devouring
Her eyes swam-
Like dark locust things,

An opulent sarcophagus her beguiling stature
In her vault my character defaced
A hopeless suspension shackled by lust
Condemned to tunnels and windows of dust,

A pathetic mummification crawling with
Insects, Because of her pestilent beauty I am
Encased,   Eternally wrapped by her burial sight,
Yet content to be blind-
I am Pharaoh!

J. Munro Jr.

LAKESIDE MORNING

First light shear optical trance
        Then sequin blue lake side dance
Sandcastles disappearing into the core
Memory of her upon blue wind floor,
Orange silk-like motion caressing the sun
Silhouettes glistening like a carousel begun,
Holding sand like rivers of thought
        Sliding through that which we sought
Her sensual embodiment harmoniously detached
Her imprint in waves,

Wind song whispering
Her voice still mingles with the tide
        A ship vacant sailed the horizon
The lost crew of dreamers cried,

Their sorrow felt like chill from glaziers
Appeared sketches wandering through trees
Shipwrecked in awareness we listened
Sailors solemn nautical breeze-

Observed Dream Movement: Zone

We knew......................We sighed....................................

The lighthouse stands like memories anchored
Crying mist for the early day
Like me watching ghost-ships drift
Like when woodwind schooners sailed this bay,

Through turquoise reef and her wind swept hair
We watched the fog fade-away out there
Our kiss anchored in the mist of mind
Our kiss anchored in the mist of mind,

This fathomless beacon,
               This density without time.

J. Munro Jr.

ILLUMINATED ALLEY

Behind incandescent veneer
Cinder and asphalt dwell
She ignites vagrant rebellion
Simmering back alley swell,

Vodka and mingling chaos burning slang all day
Twilight and street jazz cool the heat
Her illuminated darkness refreshes survivors
      Alley drifters work her ambiguous beat,

      Behind crucible shadows they roll the dice
Spontaneous rebels self combust
Tempestuous alley a champaign sunset
      Thread of glass
      Broken pieces unto Beggars,

Neon fragments

      Shattered trust.

Observed Dream Movement: Zone

MOONLIGHT TRUCKER

Nothing will change, the sun will rise
Spinning hubcaps enhance his white line trance
    Jukebox nostalgia his roadhouse sanctuary
      Tail lights shape-shift his moonlight romance,

If she is alone when he gets home suspicion will sleep
Home life recollection of their promise unfulfilled,
But the diesel's mantra rumbles through his head
Their domestic white noise fantasy
All but dead,

The night road is a fragmented sojourn moon
Truckers spurn lunar orchards with midnight steel,
Convoy conversation lively from cab to cab
    Daylight spurns his incarnate wheel,

    Undetected by sleepy travelers
To the sleeping masses a fractured life unreal,
Nothing will change the sun will set
Spinning hubcaps re-awaken his Samurai wheel,

His moonlight sanctuary
Roadhouse Bastille
His rumbling incarnate Samurai wheel.

Observed Dream Movement: Zone

MOONLIGHT HITCHHIKER
(A sympathetic ear)

Weary truck driver approaching exit
        Night camouflaged terrain, his pain
A gilded starlight trapeze
Through pores of smog pretentious neon web
Smokestack emulsions assimilate headlamp specters,
Campground pilgrim follows moonlit tread,

On the road caleco
On the road alone
Hitchhiker
Walking vagabond
On the highway the Earth
        Through the universe
The trees   Warm breeze
Pavement recycled vibrant cloak-
Brain stem mistress rolls on,

J. Munro Jr.

In the cab on the short-wave
        Straw Dog and Road Island Red they said,
Speaking of stray wives like cats
Camouflaged in the terrain of loneliness
DIVORCE
In morning exhaust after nine years! Nine lives,

Eight on the road.

Observed Dream Movement: Zone

CHRISTMAS MORNING REFLECTION

Like Christmas morning
Flame
Deep and Continuous
Below North Star Cathedral
Sacred glowing light,

During Christmas morning flurry
Inner wrappings crackling
Fireplace, boxes and brand new ties,
Concealed paramours, her memory reflecting
Gifts reflect her adulterous lies.

                                        Creepy

J. Munro Jr.

BASIS OF MY REALITY

Beyond excruciating pain beyond every single twitch
In the space where I rest after finding my niche,
Where fantasies pale
Infatuation can't deceive
Where all great moments gain strength
Giving more than they receive,

You are with me every single morning
Where heartfelt pages find
A brilliant rainbow through clouds
Your smile brings to mind,

I love you is not a hardcover statement
Or relative cliché,
It is the foundation of life,
More than anyone can say,

You are my fundamental source
Without reason or confusion
You are my breath and my freedom
Not related to evolution,

Observed Dream Movement: Zone

I love you,
My rainbow daughter-Stefani
My sons-Jimmy and Chris.

Adding to this wonderful tree of interdependence
With admiration, love and respect
My beautiful grandchildren- Mariah and James
My beautiful pseudo daughter-in-law-Chelsea.

OBSERVED- MLK'S DREAM MOVEMENT

Awoken from dream I observed his transcendence
Outside deja-vu window social equality seemed near,
During earthbound gaze in third eye luminosity
His inner strength and wisdom were suddenly so clear;

His spirit soaring like surreal bliss
His declaration profound
Astral travel like freedom enchanting
His unified society is coming around,

In crystal voidness garden eclipse
His illusory body shining like full moon sight,
Like a bewildering ethereal brilliance
Bellowing passionate shadow bright,

Lucid his movement the martyred King
Spellbound prophet in euphoric flight
Stardust portrait supernatural projection
His universal message inspiring-

Draped by cumulus night.

This poem is a reconfiguration in support of Black Lives Matter

I always try to remain mindful of the fact that All Lives Matter. (2020)

.

CHAPTER THREE

Poetic Commentaries citing religious
Historical and scriptural doctrine in addition to
Impressions related to the latent archipelago of
Zone

Observed Dream Movement: Zone

HERETIC WIND

Heretic wind prophecy proliferated
Judas hanging from Christian faith throne
God planned Judas's suicidal betrayal
Or the body of Christ-
Archaeology's bone,

God used him,
        God needed him
God pushed him to the edge to fulfill his biblical dream
        God blessed the others with Sainthood
        God damned Judas with guilt/Judas chose Lucifer's
gallows
Judas hangs above Hell Fire Stream,

Da Vinci's Last Supper blood grail of deceit
Michelangelo's ceiling an inverted pagan floor
The absolute truth supported by scripture-
Of this premeditated act to Christianity I implore;
        End this travesty
               End this tragedy

J. Munro Jr.

Allow his exclusion from Sainthood NO MORE!
Allow Judas's exclusion from Sainthood NO MORE!
JUDAS DESERVES SAINTHOOD

>We want Judas
>>We want Judas

FOREVER..

Observed Dream Movement: Zone

THE ORTHODOX NEST

Sistine gargoyles cower in this dungeon seam
With the destruction of bone
Paralyzing scream
Reptiles ingest serenity
A slithering taste for torture across stone
Jaundiced red eyed priests
Cloaked stalkers unearthly drone,

Hooded cathedral procession
Vacant brood unkind
Anal punishment quenched centuries perverse
Excretions palatable to bestial swine,

Hideous creature wielding Spear of Destiny
With skillful religious strokes severs human torso
The war ignoramus frenzied
Theological thugs torment lepers
The ruthless Viper proclaims The New Testament absolute;

PRAISE THE BLOOD BANNER!

Or crawl,
Devil snakes will squeeze the Exodus,

Pelicans appear
Mute visceral fear
Alone
So alone
Iron cross branded pain,

Like sacred dagger mutilation
Glorified sin taints the Biblical nest
Gnostic Brethren beaten and burnt,
Genocide of purity the Orthodox quest.

Observed Dream Movement: Zone

CRUSADE

Rapacity grows wicked
Vengeful violence from foul Messiah's rage
Messengers of God marching cancerous revelation,
Church Lords erect-
Gospel peasant whores parade,

In spacious bowel their Holy Covenant wasted
Feudal demons defile logic and equality
Conservative tyrants ominously ascend
Their righteous crusade a shameless charade,

Mutant guardians swollen
Predatory kingdoms emulate inquisition
Besieged Templars sought splintered cross
Benign Grail
Labyrinth
Crucified dawn,

Blood-red fissures swallowed desert motif
Scorched fury wraith-like storm
Ignoble Crusade overwhelmed windblown

J. Munro Jr.

Sand-

Like grains of war.

THE INQUISITION

Sadistic disciples cold
Spiritual chamber bare
Witches by scripture arrogance burnt
The Papacy flaunted sanctimonious lair,

Impure dogma exhilarating
Masochistic believers gnaw rosary chain
Incisors ordained impaled the playful children,

Lucifer's passion a fiery wing prayer
Perpetual rape their red hot addiction
Stigmata's masquerade a blistering mirage
Mirrors reflect stained glass inferno,

Inquisition ungodly like mask of Incubus
Seductive evil penetrating orgy
Cranium engorged obscenity
Enamored phallic choking horned flamingos
A vile silhouette flaming,

J. Munro Jr.

Demonic mass
Demented nest
Hideous dance in the domain of incest,
Diabolical beings
Deformed tongue beast
Voracious tool ripping inflicted gash
Captive womb festering
Maggots cloistered in raw placenta;

The fertile haven looms-
In seminary of filth.

IN HYPOCRITES DOMAIN
(Christian Trump voters)

Christian hypocrites
Pagans reborn
Proclamation from scorned legion sage,
Moist dungeon sharp
Abominations buried secret
Russians manipulate Trump voter puppets,
Confederates attack from Trump voter's stage,

The sweatshop fuehrer's diseased confession
Fecal varices oozing scent
Trump pets canonize minority oppression
The heart of the truth seeker slandered and caged,

"Mexico will pay" their everyday lie
"No global warming" brain washes fools
Republican health care a hoax unlike Covid
Hypocrites rant against Due-Process rule;
"Throw her in jail!"
"Throw Hillary in jail!"
The resurrection of Hitlers gas chamber tool!!

J. Munro Jr.

In the evangelist's tabernacle obstructive psalms rewind
Their practice of faith like dung beetles working
Christianity's eulogy their parable muffled
Their glorification of God-

Like laughter.

THE CRAZY REPUBLICAN SCALPEL

Political rhetoric hovering in upper extremities connects with fibrous abstract formations and blatant schizophrenia. Lines and curves extend from orbitals into eternity sending non-essential currents back to the perpetual pendulum causing known shapes to decorticate into unrecognizable designs while avant-garde fibers tingle with delight. Racial colors fill empty spaces between biased membranes nourishing dangling personalities unable to formulate a simple mathematical sequence because of extreme low-self esteem festering in anal retentive tissue. In some of us compassionate fluids flow in these cavities enabling one to observe the systematic shredding of freedom and the face of Democracy being cut into disproportionate layers. That is, the observance of how the fascist GOP ignores the pursuit of equality and uses the Electoral College to dissect the will of the people.

Check several sites on the internet to see what they vote and stand for. The last two republican presidents lost the popular vote.
2020 jmjr.

J. Munro Jr.

LAKE LAWYER SUICIDE

A bird
An eagle
A mind,

Lost in a cave caught
A God-fearing professional searching for acceptance
The Points of Paradise a beautiful place
Clean dirt raked hedges
Geometric blades of grass-manicured
Streets lined with ceramic flamingos
White picket fence brand new
Fertile skies synthetic blue
Picturesque sailing water ride
Romantic trips smother suicide,

A lawyer debating the points of suicide
In handsome adornments and gospel attire
Lost on Sunday mornings,
Lost in a cave caught-
Drove from baptism into the waters of despair,

Observed Dream Movement: Zone

A bird
A flamingo

A mind with ceramic wings.

PHILOSOPHY I
(The ultimate goal of science)

It can be said that all things we know to absolutely and universally exist are physical in nature.

That is the only phenomenon that ABSOLUTELY exists that has physical properties.

THEREFORE; For God to exist god must have physical properties because all things that are known to ABSOLUTELY and universally exist have physical properties.

THEREFORE; For God to be accepted as absolutely and universally existent, science must prove God's existence by the scientific method.

THEREFORE; Because the scientific method identifies and proves physical properties, and as the capabilities of science and technology advance, through the process of extrapolation we can surmise that at some point in the future science will be able to identify and prove the existence of God because if we ABSOLUTELY know that God exists God must have physical properties.

THEREFORE; If God exists God has physical properties because all things that we ABSOLUTELY know to exist have physical properties and if the physical properties of God are identified and proven through the scientific method all will have to accept God's existence.

THEREFORE; The ultimate question for the scientific community must be does God exist because proving God's existence will have profound implications concerning all hypotheses and theories concerning life and the universe.

THEREFORE; The ultimate hypothesis for the scientific community must be "God Exists" because proving God's existence will have profound implications concerning all hypotheses and theories concerning life and the universe.

THEREFORE; Because proof of God's existence will have ultimate and profound implications concerning all hypotheses and theories concerning life and the universe the ultimate goal of science must be to prove the existence of God, being that all things we ABSOLUTELY know to exist are physical in nature.?

PHILOSOPHY II
(Unknown equivalents)

If God does not have physical properties then God cannot be proven or known to exist by the scientific method.

THEREFORE; God cannot be absolutely and universally known to exist because all things absolutely and universally known to exist must be proven to exist by the scientific method.

THEREFORE; If God exists without having physical properties a person must have faith that God exists because God's existence cannot be known or proven by the scientific method.

THEREFORE; If God's existence cannot be known or proven by the scientific method, having faith that God exists is having faith that an unknown exists.

Premise; ALL PHENOMENA THAT CANNOT BE PROVEN TO EXIST BY THE SCIENTIFIC METHOD ARE EQUALLY UNKNOWN.

THEREFORE; Having faith that an unknown exists is equivalent to having faith that all other unknowns exist because all unknowns are equally unknown.

THEREFORE; Having faith that an unknown exists is speculating that a particular unknown exists based on abstract or non-proven concepts and conjecture.

THEREFORE; All religions, philosophies and hypotheses have faith and offer speculation that a particular unknown exists or at least might exist.

THEREFORE; If one unknown is equivalent to all other unknowns it must be acknowledged that all religions, philosophies and hypotheses based on faith and conjecture are equally unknown.

THEREFORE; If all religions, philosophies and hypotheses are equally unknown there can be no argument or conflict between them because all unknown quantities are equally unknown. Debating which is true or not is no different than trying to separate a heterogeneous solution containing holy water and sewer water. Only to find out that you can't distinguish one from the other.

MUTE SPIDERS TEACH HEALTH CARE

Some of my thoughts are like asteroids or comets. Once in a while I come up with a great idea or concept and it speeds with magnificent brightness across the blank infinity of my mind. Just as quickly it disappears. It rarely reappears. Almost never when I want it or need it for some big ego reason. When they do reoccur out of nowhere, for no reason at all, I remain mute.

I am not afraid of spiders, I am afraid of pain I am not afraid of dying, I am afraid of pain

If I was not afraid of pain what would I be afraid of? Would I be afraid of nothing? Does nothing even exist? If so nothing would be something..............................

Buddhism teaches the mind how not to respond to all non altruistic and non benevolent thoughts. It is taught that this skill allows beneficial and positive behavior to flourish in a world of mediocrity.

Buddha taught meditation 500 years before Christ. Psychology and the medical community now claim meditation to be a legitimate method for improving mental and physical wellness. And that it is advisable to practice this newly proven and unique method of health care.

All good, Buddha's thought
2001 jmjr.

BUDDHIST/EXISTENTIAL DICHOTOMY

"I think therefore I am"*
I am therefore I am not,

"I think therefore I am"
    I am therefore I think
    I think therefore I understand
    I understand therefore I realize
    I realize therefore I actualize
    I actualize therefore I become
    I become therefore I am,
I am therefore I am not.

* Rene Descartes

REUNION OF MENAGERIE

Solstice pageantry celebrates prey
Draining mantle casket unblessed
Thirsting apostle spinal frame
Cachectic virgin waiting in shame,
Violent memorial
Gothic courtyard madman
Heathens practicing taboo remain,

Sacrifice torn by tattooed assassin
Nefarious burial in negligee of gloom
Hedonistic debutante her orifice necrotic
A decayed cemetery

CARNIVAL OF DOOM

Immolation feast for the devout
Ignorance plague debauchery's contagion
Thrusting
Vine-noose like fetish
Across purulent floor clammy thorned-
Menagerie,

Inhabitants of dusk squeal, steal and plunder
Barbaric incantations invoke species infirm
Restless tower mottled-Bodily fluids clinging
Venomous Devas rupture flailing copious
flesh,

Viscous footprints roam graveyard montage
Carnal missionaries climbing
stairs
In the house with mongrels creeping revival
Above pounding drums cyclic chatter
The circle of bondage a trenchant bond-
Dominate like hunter,
Then fallen like prey.

Observed Dream Movement: Zone

E.R.
(White Room Trauma)

In White Room of Tragic Spells
Crimson pentagrams attune
Post Mortem embalming malignancy
  Perimeter drama insidious trauma
Creed, Austere wrath of death Hovering-
Sanguinary etiquette   Symbolic
God-like beings feed,

Where spiraling barriers collide
Fatally torn her severed womb
While cast then in voodoo bane
We tried to warm her bled out tomb,

Pearl gate mediators transience judge
I sensed their intentions as a friend
A white room for bewildered souls
Their merciful choice not to mend,

J. Munro Jr.

In the fountain of trauma bloodless tissues die
After self-pity tranquility humbles sin
After lucid horror then brutal struggle bleak
Like a gentle rain she approached me from behind
Like lilac wings across newborn skin
With the appreciation of a loving daughter she kissed my cheek,

In an aerial cloud so lofty
With loving kindness so gentle
So gently-
        She kissed my cheek.

Observed Dream Movement: Zone

FULL CODE
(Her Last Dance)

Perplexed by abrupt anoxia
Her "Helter Skelter" image askew
Her pale expressionless prayer quivering
A wrinkled life consumed,

The Dancing Rag Doll's existential encore;

We worked to restore her worn out re-appearance
Like rewarming a riddled coal burning Honky Tonk
Injecting fuel
Checking for heat
No spark-no miracle
No curtain call this time

Her fright unseen /wine glass cataracts unmoved

Her pain dried tears-unknown- can't find,

As attachment withered beneath her cold shapeless breasts
Leaving the worn out cadaver like from orgasm into
afterglow

J. Munro Jr.

Her spirit danced,
Then thunderous crowd-afterlife staircase
White Marble Ballroom

SUCHNESS

Ethereal assembly a nondual order
Pastels of awareness cleanse catacomb of tears
Vapors from blissful galleries suffocate religion
Truth unaffected by deception of fears,

Like Jesus's manifesto salvation affirmed
Innate Suchness euphoric factor of Death
Imploding ego eroding rust
The cohesive nature of compassion-
Inherent within us,

Through Redwood canopy higher powers emanate
Like towering streams of sunlight bliss
Beneath Redwood canopy we vacillate toward Suchness
Like sparrows flying through morning power line zone
Like through residue of ten billion suns.

J. Munro Jr.

SOMEWHERE

Something not lost not to be found
Distant constellations adorn matrix called Christ
Between here and there cloud drift provides shelter
Restless memories agonize destiny's approach
Approaching again, the perpetual rogue chill
Loneliness   Solemn wall of hope,

Holy sinister organisms coping with gravity
Replicants populate silicone anthills
Aliens serenade in palatial wormholes-
 Like angel reliquary
Moonlit gardens form shapeless temple
Alchemic mercenaries construct artificial nations
Robots fertilize the internet frontier,

Digital Yaqui translate petroglyphs
Self-awareness not unlike tumble weed called God
Not unlike peyote turn style somewhere
Somewhere bacteria spore
Falling leaves disappear
In the frozen rings of Saturn
Or the Asteroid Belt
Or in another sub-atomic explosion.

PSYCHIC VISION

Cognitive empires vaporize like precious metal
Iconic flashes turn metallic sky
Ornate cosmos vague stealth-like perception
Cumulus stratosphere nebulous
Psychic vision high,

Mercurial village like fabric unwoven
Silver lagoon spools
Embroidered patterns faraway territories
Bending unhinged fences,
Autumn's parasol twirling
Twisting braids fibrous gold
Premonitions chasing silos
Crop circle haze
Time traveler's prophecies unfold,
Heaven's brittle framework absent
Paintings of herbivores climbing
Scenic images from fairy tales yet told,

J. Munro Jr.

Casey's continent in future's past
Smoldering battle field's burnt blood in passing
Elastic streets stretched in places
Plastic bottle neck faces
Serendipitous fortunes variegate the hourglass season
Fuzzy green spirals penetrating eyelid caverns
Steel monument tunnels Artifact
Pastures.

UNITY

Unlike creation in Genesis
Collage of Angels and Dakinis unite galactic array
Spectacular panorama of parallel origination
Vibrant particles elucidating space
Holes
            Esoteric halo,

Failing worlds idolize pantheons of myth
Moments of realization dwarf fortress called
Earth Formless concepts expand
Stagnant systems collapse
Windmill lullabies hush incubating prairies
Absolute plush grange,

Borders between Gods cellophane blue
Non gravitational phase the palisade of tomorrow
Holograms unify virtual alignment

Akashic Sheppard's cryptic trail

Intrinsic walking at 4:00 a.m.-

How dark matter is the glue of the universe-
Compassion is to humanity.
The greater the fear the greater the wisdom,
The greater the happiness, the greater the wisdom.

Observed Dream Movement: Zone

HIMALAYAN STARLIGHT

Shrines of antiquity intertwine
Buddha's pendant/prayer wheel vine
Ancient oracles elusive crossing,
The Occult Archipelago,

India's lamp a Hindu chateau
        Guru's pyre boundless
Incense
Altruistic source blossoming
        Sphere with scented eons,

Snow cap realm like Aurora dazzling
        Zen garden fluorescent
            Kathmandu,   Pine trees sway
Valley of Insight   Tibetan landscape
Meditation in view
        Dharma wisdom
Lingering
        Tantric Deities,

J. Munro Jr.

When Buddhist stupas evaporate
Himalayan starlight mystifying moon
      Lamas contemplate Nirvana's wavelength
      Chakra disc and lotus bloom,

Juxtaposed clear mountain Avatars levitate,

              Yoginis fly......

Observed Dream Movement: Zone

SIMPLE THOUGHT
Sprinkled with Synonyms

blah blah
Ob-La-Life Goes On-Da
Beatology

Many years ago I came across what I consider to be the most accurate and profound definition of love that I have ever heard. I read it in a Buddhist text written by a Buddhist monk from somewhere under the Himalayan star light. I cannot remember which text or the name of the monk, but I have never forgotten the quote; "Love is a feeling of oneness with someone or something without attachment, clinging, desire, lust, happiness, sadness, envy, jealousy or anger". This was not your typical "A Day In A Life" moment for me. Unexpectedly, while reading these simple "Words of Love" I fell into a "Sargent Peppers Lonely Heart Club" trance. I felt like I was standing in a gentle "Rain". But when a vibrant "Carnival of Light' began to radiate through my "Long Long Long" nervous system I knew this was going to be one of those crazy "Day Tripper" experiences. I felt like I was "Flying". It was better than "A Taste of Honey". The excitement did not stop there. After a few minutes, before I could say "Good Day Sunshine" "I Saw Her Standing There". Wanting to "Act Naturally" I tried to regain my composure as quickly as possible. But without warning "She Came In Through The Bathroom Window". She was like a wild "Child Of Nature". I thought holy cow I've "Got To Get You Into My Life". "I'm In Love". I lost all control. Feeling "Free As A Bird" a "Real Love" impulse abruptly burst into my elusive "Sun King" synapse. It was then that "Lucy In The Sky" took me down to "Strawberry Fields Forever". Wow, "Love Me Do" and do not "Ask Me Why" but never "In My Life" have I experienced anything like that!, I said to myself. Once re-orientated from this brief journey with the "Magical Mystery Tour" the thought came to me that this simple definition of love can be paraphrased as such; love is a feeling of oneness with "other" without attachment, desire, anger, etc. "Etcetera".

Remaining in the "Octopus's Garden" I continued to be mesmerized by the "Glass Onion" effects of the Beatorium from which I could not leave with "No Reply". After what seemed to be "A Hard Day's Night" I soon realized that it was time to "Get Back". While trying to decide whether to call for "Help" or just getting a "Ticket To Ride" I distinctly overheard "Mean Mister Mustard" tell "Lovely Rita" that even money "Can't Buy Me Love". "Like Dreamers Do" I felt "Misery" after hearing this "I'm Down" "I'm A Loser" kind of "Junk". It occurred to me that this guy just might be the real "Fool On The Hill". After "Fixing A Hole" I began to think that things were "Getting Better". I then said to myself O.K., I think "I'll follow The Sun". This unusual and for me a rare "I Feel Fine" occasion led me down "The Long and Winding Road". While walking down the "Blue Jay Way" the thought came to me that "It Won't Be Long" until my thoughts "Come Together". "It Won't Be Long" until I realize the ultimate definition of love. Which I did. "I Want To Tell You" strictly "From Me To You" that this echo can be heard every "Now And Then" throughout Buddhist doctrine. While "While My Guitar Gently Weeps" resonated somewhere "Across The Universe" this profound rendition appeared like a "Here Comes The Sun" moment and is stated simply as such; Love is Oneness. Period! This realization was "Something" like a "Revolution". Along with the reminder that "It's Only Love" I came to understand that the central theme while in this simple state of mind was that the original Buddhist definition of love was made simpler by using "other" as a synonym for the pronouns someone and something. Never "In My Life" did I ever "Imagine" that "This Boy" would come up with such a thought. It seems like it just happened "Yesterday". This simple narrative is an introductory examination of the term "other" and a brief and simple comparative between the Buddhist and the traditional western interpretations of what is implied or meant by the concept of love.

Based on the Oxford Dictionary's definition of other it is sufficient to say that other does not include or imply the pronouns I, us, we, one or oneself. We will call this collection of pronouns the "non-other" factors. Based on the Oxford Dictionary's definition of other, for the purposes specific to this narrative, we will consider(for now) "other" to be synonymous with the pronouns you, someone, something, everyone, and everything. Allowing for this selective definition of "other" my simplified Buddhist definition of love is plausible. For example, supported by the associative principle, in view of these definitions of love and "other" if we say that we love someone or something we are saying that we love "other" and if we love "other" we also love everyone and everything because everyone and everything are also synonymous with "other". From this point on, based on this simple presumption we will envision "other" as a categorical synonym that includes someone, something, everyone, and everything.

Keeping this simple categorical synonym called "other" in mind and not meaning to over complicate this simple exposition, it is now necessary for me to introduce the Buddhist concept of Emptiness. In simple terms Buddhist philosophy states that ALL phenomena, all things that exist in the physical and metaphysical realms possess the same ultimate nature. This ultimate nature is called Emptiness (Science also claims that all matter, all phenomena in the universe consists of ultimate components such as electrons, neutrinos etc. And ultimately a more "fundamental phenomenon yet to be identified")(1). For me it is interesting to note that both Buddhist philosophy and science acknowledge that all phenomena possess a universal fundamental nature. To me the questions then arise; Does science support Buddhism? Do these parallel concepts of ultimate reality converge? Regardless, both disciplines concur that all objects are of the same marrow. For example, based on this Buddhist/Science construct of an ultimate essence a house is the same as a car. My ultimate metaphysical/physical nature is the same as yours and both of us possess the same fundamental nature that embodies all existents and phenomena in the universe(s). (Again, this is a very simplistic explanation of Emptiness).

As we continue this simple dialog, at this point it is now necessary to expand our definition of "other." For this narrative, the concept/word of emptiness will now be included in the definition of "other." Henceforth the expanded definition of "other" will be; "other" is the collection of pronouns that includes someone, something, everyone, everything, and emptiness. As we evolve along this line of thinking when saying I have a feeling of oneness with someone or something, that is, I have a feeling of oneness with "other" we are also implying that I have feeling of oneness with emptiness because as shown emptiness is synonymous with "other". (Further on emptiness will be considered to be a proxy for our informal mandate of the yet to be introduced definition of "Buddhist Other") It is crucial to have a basic comprehension of emptiness to understand the Buddhist definition of love because this is where the Buddhist and the traditional western interpretations of love diverge. Up to this point our explanations and understanding of love have been based on western vocabulary, concepts, and beliefs. Putting the Buddhist concept of emptiness into the admix changes the perspective.

It is taught that for one to understand the definition and to experience Buddhist love one must remember that emptiness is the ultimate nature of ALL phenomena. In view of this narrative only, when this concept is fathomed, one must then accept that emptiness is a synonym of "other"(someone, something, everything, etc.). Once that is assimilated it must then be understood that if emptiness is the ultimate nature of all phenomena emptiness must be the ultimate nature of the "non other" pronouns stated above as well. For one to grasp the relevance of these concepts in view of this narrative one must now think in these terms; Being that emptiness is the ultimate nature of all phenomena, emptiness is not only the ultimate nature of "other" but also the ultimate nature of the "non-other" factors(I,me,us,we). Emptiness is synonymous with ALL those pronoun factors. It is imperative to understand that emptiness is synonymous with both "other" and "non-other" factors. Emptiness unifies "other" and "non-other." With this graduated indulgence in mind, we must now extrapolate from the definition of the expanded "other." We will call the new expanded definition of "other" the "Buddhist other." "Buddhist other" is just what we have mentioned above. It is the unification of "other and the "non-other" factors. Because "other", "non-other" and emptiness are by definition terms that define "Buddhist other" we can say that all these factors are synonymous. By invoking the associative principle once again we will restate this equation of synonyms as "other" plus "non-other" are synonyms of emptiness, (O+NOF=E). With this equation in mind we can now make the innovative generalization that "Buddhist other" is ALL-INCLUSIVE because is incorporates all factors of "other" "non-other" and emptiness (BO=O+NOF+E). (Note: BO is not to be confused with BS). For simplicity's sake we will use the synonym empty(E) to refer to the collection of these synonymous factors (BO).

Given this very liberal latitude, from the Buddhist mindset to say that love is a feeling of oneness with "other" is the same as saying that love is a feeling of oneness with everyone, a feeling of other with "other", a feeling of oneness with emptiness, etc., etc., etc. To those who faithfully subscribe to the dogmatic western constructs of love the question can easily arise; How can this be true? It sounds ridiculous. If I love someone how can I love everyone etc., etc.? One reason this question emerges in the western psyche is because it is our habitual inclination to think that love is a personal attachment to a specific someone(s) or something(s). This habitual predisposition occurs because the western precepts of love evolve around the "non-other" concept of "I." I love this or that exclusively. To the western mind love is a self-centered declaration claiming emotional ownership or exclusive unity with its selected object(s). Because of this narrow singularity it is natural for the western mind to believe that the Buddhist definition of love is no more than a Disney fairy tale that is unobtainable in reality. From the western mindset this "other"/empty kind of love is out of touch. How can love be a state of mind that includes everything? "It's All Too Much". In contrast, it is because Buddhist philosophy considers emptiness to be an ALL-INCLUSIVE concept that the Buddhist definition of love is not only credible but is in actuality a primordial or pre-embryonic state of consciousness.

Because Buddhist philosophy teaches that everything

is "empty of inherent existence"(2) these interpretations of Buddhist love and our definition of "other" are valid. At least from the Buddhist perspective. What this means is that when contemplating or experiencing this love one is abiding in the all-inclusive state of emptiness(oneness or "other"). When contemplating or experiencing this state of love there are no borders between concepts, feelings, phenomenon, or vocabulary. Everything(E) is a synonym! Something is nothing therefore nothing is something.

To comprehend this condition, in part, it must be construed that the initial referent of Buddhist love, as with all concepts of love, is "I/me". But here it must be remembered that the Buddhist concept of I/me is synonymous with "other"(E) and therefore the thought of "I/me" is the thought or experience of emptiness. In Buddhist love "I" must always be thought of as a synonym of emptiness. Based on this formality it can be shown that from the Buddhist perspective the western interpretations of "I" and love are but allusions. From the Buddhist perspective, because emptiness is an all-inclusive state of mind there are no reference points to distinguish or separate "I" from the other factors of "other"(E).

To say the words, "I love" has the same meaning as saying "other" love or empty love. Again, this is because in Buddhist philosophy "other" and the non-other factors(I, me etc.) are equivalent in creed. It must also be pointed out that when experiencing this state of love the feelings of attachment, desire, lust etc. become synonyms of (E) "Buddhist other" as well. To re-quote; Love is a feeling of oneness with someone or something WITHOUT attachment, desire, jealousy, lust, anger etc. Buddhist literature implies that when experiencing Buddhist love all those feelings are synonyms of (E). The element of emptiness causes those feelings to be thought of or experienced as (E). Those feelings are empty as well. That's all. Because Emptiness(E) manifests when experiencing Buddhist love, no internal dialog can arise to support the existence of those feelings. One just abides in the state of emptiness (E)without acknowledging or even being aware of those emotions.

When one is contemplating or experiencing Buddhist love "I" is the same as emptiness(E). The first thought of "I" is the apprehension of emptiness. Saying I am is the same as saying you are, someone is, "other" is etc. They are all empty. The main idea is that all these pronouns have the same connotation, the same meaning. They are synonyms! It is that simple. Period! There is no subject or object. Just oneness or emptiness. Buddhist psychology(3) describes this condition, this moment of love as a state of perception without conceptualization and explains it to be similar to what a newborn baby might experience when first introduced to the sensory world or like the state of non conceptual awareness when experiencing a moment of thoughtless thought while standing on a beautiful beach overlooking the clear blue ocean horizon. This state of mind dwells in a world where all concepts have been assimilated into the single word/concept called emptiness. All is empty! It is that simple! When experiencing this introspective boundless moment one experiences an inexpressible feeling of bliss and joy that surpasses what can be experienced through what is considered to be a narrow egocentric western experience of love because as we have shown western love is based on the limiting concept of "I". That is the private "I". The "I" that is exclusively a "non- other" pronoun. It has been said that this private "I" can not enter or even begin to comprehend the unrestricted intimacy inherent to the all inclusive, inexpressible state of emptiness(E).

To try and clarify this comparison between the inherent concepts of Buddhist love and some of the western ideas of love I will briefly elucidate some of the ideals and practices included under the umbrella of western love. Included are the sanctity of marriage and divorce, monogamous and polygamist intimate relationships. The acceptance and support for Trump's sweatshops. The love and support for the greedy and inconsiderate policies and practices that support the oppression of a multitude of humanity by denying and or limiting their human right to receive healthcare without being put into the unsettling, unfair position of having to hope and beg for charity. In other words, the love and support for the "Christian/Repub" morality that justifies stripping others of their dignity. There are many more but I would like to mention the practice of love and support for the denials and lies about there being no global warming. To have done and to continue to do so is and will be harmful to our children and grandchildren because they won't be ready for it. My regression into politics was not intended, but the examples given are applicable to this discussion and it just seemed appropriate at the time.

Moving forward, in contrast to "western love" the state of mind called emptiness can be thought of as universal love, a state of oneness with "other". Buddhist philosophy teaches that there are two truths. One is called duality or the relative truth. Buddhist psychology considers this to be our normal way of interpreting sensory input and thoughts. And our way of expressing and understanding these experiences. The other truth is called non-duality or the ultimate truth. This can be described as a state of mind that does not discriminate between sensory input or thoughts. All experiences, all phenomena are viewed as a continuity of the condition of oneness, "other" or in terms of Buddhism, all experiences are empty. Further discussion of emptiness/

non-duality is well beyond the purpose of this narrative and my very limited understanding of it. If any of this narrative strikes a cord I encourage you to pursue the investigation and study of Buddhism. Thankfully there are many books, CD's and centers of information available, especially on the internet.

In conclusion, if we could/would attain this state of mind called emptiness(E, "other", etc.), or at least try to internalize it to some degree I believe it would be possible for us to gain insight into the minds of Abraham, Buddha, Gandhi, Jesus, Lincoln, Mohamed and so on. I believe it would be possible for us to experience their mind of selflessness and therefore better understand their world- changing ideologies. It would be possible to experience if for only an instant, the how and why they did what they did. What helped them persevere until the actualization of their altruistic goals. What factors influenced their decisions. What motivated them to initiate and pursue their dangerous and often life threatening tasks. By obtaining this ultimate state, if only for a second, it is my belief we would come to understand that these inspirational, selfless, otherwise typical beings achieved their particular altruistic attainments because they were motivated by the feeling of oneness with "other-E"(everyone, everything). I believe that by approaching this level of insight and compassion we would come to the realization that all beings inherently possess this capacity and therefore have the potential to attain and sustain this level of love, this state of oneness, emptiness. By following "The Inner Light" we would come to understand that the essence of "other" is intuitive, originating well beyond the prelinguistic(3) level.

The acquisition of this knowledge does have a down side. I believe comprehension of this Utopian panacea would augment the indubitable and disheartening fact that the only way world peace can ever come to pass is if everyone in the world were to develop this feeling of oneness with "other". That the only way world peace can be actualized is if all beings embrace this ultimate zone called emptiness. By possessing this knowledge one would come to know that emptiness(E) impales the holy grail and purges the earth-rot illusions of love and ego. One would know that the state of (E) makes transparent the undeniable truth that world peace can not be realized until ALL people come to the heartfelt realization that "All Things Must Pass" so just "Let It Be".

To summarize by invoking Beatle-isms one more time; "Dear Prudence" please remember that when taking a slow walk down "Penny Lane" "All You Need Is Love" and that "There Is A Place" where the "Nowhere Man" can proclaim, "We Can Work It Out"! Or in the spirit of this narrative;

"ALL TOGETHER NOW"

NOTES/REFERENCES

Note- Other than "other" and the quoted definition of Buddhist love all quoted words and phrases are TITLES of Beatles songs;

Beatles. "Act Naturally." *Help*. Parlophone/Capitol Records. 1965. Movie/Album Beatles. "Across the Universe." *White Album*. Apple Records.1968. Album

Beatles. "A Day In A Life." *Sgt. Pepper's Lonely Heart club band*. Capitol Records1967. Album. Beatles. "A Hard Day's Night." *A Hard Day's Night*. Parlophone/United Artists. 1964. Album. George Harrison. "All Things Must Pass." All Things Must Pass. Apple Records. 1970,album. Beatles. "All Together Now." *Yellow submarine*. Capitol Records/EMI. 1969. Album.

Beatles. "All You Need Is Love." *Magical* Mystery *Tour*. Parlophone/Capitol Record 1967. Album. Beatles. "Ask Me Why." *Twist And Shout*. EMI/Capitol Records. 1964. Album. Beatles. "A Taste Of Honey." *Twist and Shout*. EMI/Capitol Records. 1964. Album.

Beatles. "Can't Buy Me Love." *A Hard Day's Night*. Parlophone/United Artists. 1964. Album. McCartney, Paul. "Carnival Of Light." Unreleased . 1967.

Lennon, John, Beatles. " Child Of Nature." Unreleased 1968.
Beatles. "Come Together." *Abbey Road*. Apple Records. 1969. Album. Beatles. "Day Tripper." *Yesterday and Today*. Capitol Records. 1966. Album. Beatles. "Dear Prudence." *The Beatles*. Apple Records. 1968. Album McCartney, Paul. "Etcetera." Unreleased 1968.

Beatles/Lennon, John "Free As A Bird." *Anthology1/ Unreleased*. Apple/Capital R.1977/1995. Album. Beatles. "Fixing A Hole." *Sgt. Pepper's Lonely Heart Club Band*. Capitol Records. 1967. Album.

Beatles. "Fool On The Hill, The." *Magical Mystery Tour*. Parlophone/Capitol Records. 1967. Album Beatles. "From Me To You." *Twist and Shout*. EMI/Capital. 1964. Album.

Beatles. "Flying". *Magical Mystery Tour."* Parlophone/ Capitol Records. 1967. Album. Beatles. "Get Back." *Let It Be."* Apple. 1969/1970. Single/Album.

Beatles. "Glass Onion." *White Album*. Apple Records. 1968. Album.

Beatles. "Getting Better." *Sgt. Pepper's Lonely Heart Club Band*. Capitol Records. 1967. Album. Beatles. "Glass Onion." *White Album*. Apple Records.1968. Album.

Beatles. "Got To Get You Into My Life." *Revolver*. Parlophone/ EMI. 1966. Album. Beatles. "Here Comes The Sun." *Abbey Road*. Apple Records. 1969. Album.

Beatles. "Help." *Help*. Parlophone/Capitol Records. Soundtrack/album. 1965. Beatles. "I Feel Fine." Capital. 1964. Single.

Beatles. "I'm In Love." Beatles bootleg recordings. Parlophone. 1963. Beatles. "I Want To Tell You." *Revolver*. Parlophone/EMI. 1966. Album.

Beatles. "I'll Follow The Sun." *Beatles for Sale*. Parlophone/EMI. 1964. Album. Lennon, John. "Imagine." *Imagine*. Apple. 1971. Album.

Beatles. "I'm A Loser." *Beatles For Sale*. Parlophone/EMI. 1964. Album. Beatles. "I'm Down." *Help*. Parlophone/Capitol Records. 1965. Album. Beatles. "In My Life." *Rubber Soul*. Parlophone/EMI. 1965. Album

Beatles. " Inner Light, The." *White-Super Deluxe*. Apple Records. 1968. Album. Beatles. " It's All Too Much." *Yellow Submarine*. Capital/EMI. 1969. Album Beatles. "It's Only Love." *Help*. Parlophone/Capitol Record. 1965. Movie, Album. Beatles. "'It Won't Be Long." *Meet The Beatles*. Capital/EMI London. 1964. Album.

McCartney, Paul. "Junk." *McCartney*. Apple Records. 1970. Album.

Beatles/McCartney, Paul. "Like Dreamers Do." *Anthology I*, Capital/Decca/London. 1995. Album. Beatles. "Long, Long, Long." *White-Super Deluxe*. Apple Records. 1968. Album.

Beatles. "Lovely Rita." *Sgt. Pepper's Lonely Heart Club Band.* Capitol Records. 1967. Album. Beatles. "Love Me Do." *Twist and Shout.* Capitol Records/EMI. 1964. Album.

Beatles. "Lucy In The Sky." *Sgt. Pepper's Lonely Heart Club Band.* Capitol Records. 1967. Album. Beatles. "Magical Mystery Tour." *Magical Mystery Tour.* Parlophone/Capitol Records. 1967. Album. Beatles. "Mean Mr. Mustard." *Abbey Road.* Apple Records. 1969. Album.

Beatles. "Misery." *Please Please Me.* Parlophone/EMI. 1963. Album. Beatles. "No Reply." *Beatles For Sale.* Parlophone/EMI. 1964. Album. Beatles. Lennon, John. " Now And Then." Unreleased. 1978.

Beatles. "Nowhere Man." *Rubber Soul.* Parlophone/EMI. 1965. Album. Beatles. "Octopus's Garden." *Abbey Road.* Apple Records. 1969. Album.

Beatles. "Penny Lane." *Magical Mystery Tour.* Parlophone/Capitol Records. 1967. Album. Beatles. "Rain." *Hey Jude.* Apple Records. 1970. Album.

Beatles. Lennon, John. "Real Love." *Imagine/Anthology 2.* Parlophone/EMI/Apple. 1988, 1995. Beatles. "Revolution." *White-Super Deluxe.* Apple Records 1968. Album.

Beatles. "Sergeant Pepper's Lonely Heart Club Band." *Sgt. Pepper's Lonely Heart Club Band.* Capitol Records. 1967. Album.

Beatles. "She Came In From The Bathroom Window." *Abbey Road,* Apple Records. 1969. Album Beatles. "Something.". *Abbey Road.* Apple Records. 1969. Album.

Beatles. "Strawberry Fields Forever." *Magical Mystery Tour.* Parlophone/Capitol Records1967. Album. Beatles. "Sun King." *Abbey Road.* Apple Records. 1969. Album

Beatles. " There's A Place." *Please, Please Me.* Parlophone/EMI. 1963. Album. Beatles. "This Boy." *Meet The Beatles.* Capital/EMI. 1964. Album.

Beatles. "Ticket To Ride." *Help.* Parlophone/Capitol Records. 1965. Movie Album.

Beatles. "While My Guitar Gently Weeps." *White-Super Deluxe.* Apple Records. 1968. Album. Beatles. "Words Of Love." *Beatles For Sale.* Parlophone/EMI. 1964. Album.

Beatles. "Yesterday." *Help.* Parlophone/Capitol Records. 1965. Movie, Alb

*List of Beatles Songs.

1. Paulson, Steve." Roger Penrose On Why Consciousness Does Not Compute", Nautilus Science   Magazine, 2010, Issue 47.

2. Yeshe, Lama and Zopa, Lama. Wisdom Energy; Simon and Schuster, 1982.

3. Tsering, Geshe Tashi. Buddhist Psychology; Volume 3. Wisdom Publications, 2006.

CHAPTER FOUR

RIVER DEATH
(Fellowship of the Zone)

and
it's vibrant
Distributaries and tributaries,
(This chapter is a confluence
Inspired by River Death Narrative.)

RIVER DEATH
(Fellowship of the Zone)

This narrative is an attempt to describe a stranger than strange luminosity, more commonly known as a dream, and the subsequent realization that I had about it many years later. I aspired to put this dream event into words for several reasons, two of which I will state here. One was to refresh my memory of this mind-blowing experience which helps reinforce some of the beliefs and knowledge I acquired from it. Secondly, and of greater consequence, I hope it will inspire those readers who have had similar dreams, recurrent dreams, or any type of lingering impressions of time spent in kindred vestibules of clear mind (Such as those induced by psychotropics, meditation, prayer, intense study, exhaustion, orgasm or just having an innocent moment of thoughtless thought, just to name a few), to think about them from an inquisitive, non-ordinary perspective. I hope this narrative will motivate the reader(s) to follow his/her intuitive curiosity by seeking out multiple sources of information concerning the possible origins of these phenomena. If pursued with an open mind I believe one will come to see that this plethora of circumstance has a common ground. A similar basis of cause and effect. I believe sincere investigation into this "Fellowship of the Zone" will result in a dispassionate view of secular division and provide a profound newfound hope. If nothing else, it is my hope that the reader(s) will develop an intimate connection with the latent realities that lie deep within the multi-dimensional landscape of mind-knowledge. And how those realizations can result in a more pliable sense of self. I coalesce with those who support the notion that by striving to unearth one's autobiographic topography of mind one will eventually uncover the unblemished substrate from where these elusive moments emanate in wondrous assembly.

For many years this encapsulated saga remained embedded like wood rot in the uncharted depths of my subconscious. I thought of it as a haunted memory wandering the deck of a sunken galleon filled with pirate treasure and the obsessive chains of visceral addiction. Every now and then during those years of affliction I would feel its intrusive vibration pulling me toward it's fathom unknown. I could not escape its proximity or the eerie semblance that cast a disturbing apprehension across the beginningless ocean called consciousness. Unlike most dreams and memories which fade with the passing of time, the reawakening of this dream occurred with increasing reanimation and frequency. With curious reluctance I found myself thinking about it more than what seemed normal.

Contrary what "elementary" Buddhist psychological and western psychoanalytic hypotheses propose I intuitively felt that this subliminal showcase was more than an ethereal potpourri of unnoticed daily contacts intermingling with repressed childhood memory, the intoxicants of temporal desire and/or Freudian eroticism sown with fetters of lace and deviant sexuality. I had a subtle nagging urge to decipher this cauldron of metaphor. To know what this annoying curse meant. This dream was so real that I still remember some of its details and emotions conjured. It was like one of those passionate experiences that we remember and talk about or suppress deep within our secret vault of regret and inappropriate mischief.

    I consider myself to be a self-taught student of Tibetan Buddhism. An adherent of Buddhist philosophy, psychology-religion. During what was a "routine" meditation I acquired an unmistakable and profound realization about the dream. It hit me like a bolt of lightning. It reshaped my core foundation of beliefs and concepts concerning life, death, religion, science and most of all, myself. This meditative awakening was like a dream come to life which not only induced a deeper self-understanding but also tempered some of my slothful self-indulgences as well as my antagonistic cynicism regarding various behaviors and beliefs held and practiced by many individuals and societies. I feel fortunate to have had that precious mind-blowing experience. That moment arisen from the depths of "hidden treasure" is a beautiful, powerful memory.

The remainder of this narrative is presented in the classic academic research paradigm. The first segment is a descriptive explanation of the dream and the subsequent mind-state I experienced immediately after the dream. The second part is a description of the realizations during and after the meditation session which brought clarity and meaning to the dream. And finally, I will give a brief commentary concerning the content, what the dream meant to me and the ultimate capabilities and potentials I now believe can be realized through serious investigation into so called alternative ideologies and paranormal experiences.

Many believe investigation into these phenomena is imperative for psychological and spiritual development. (Note; the following is a 100% lightly embellished non-fiction memoir).

In the beginning winter arose; I still remember the unexpected adventure like it happened yesterday. Looking around it seemed as if I was mistakenly "beamed upped" into a non-galactic underworld. The aesthetic overtone was akin to Van Gogh's "Starry Night" abstraction. Not having a clue how I got there I found myself walking through a snowy woodland basin. A spectacular winter's wonderland appeared before me. There was a partially frozen river overflowing with torrential peculiarities. The gray ornate tapestry was embroidered with cumulus pastels and shimmering rays of sunlight. Auditory sensation was mute. A hollow seashell-like ambiance resonated throughout the wispy cavity of silence. My first impression was that this mercurial hideaway was nothing more than an innocuous dreamscape. While wandering this non-geographic odyssey I suddenly found myself standing at rivers edge. It was an unusual occurrence, a weird state of mind. Something like trying to imagine a space-time anomaly or maybe a clairvoyant third eye vision. At times it was confusing and optically viscous. I began wondering if I was experiencing deja vu or an obscured far-off premonition. After being preoccupied with this conundrum for a short time, as if possessed and without tangible motivation I was roused into crossing the raucous icy mosaic. My trepidation became fervent as I took several steps onto the surreal fringe of the frosted window pane canvas. In retrospect it was like I was walking into a glimmering observatory located on a psilocybin mesa in the panoptic plume of extra sensory perception. At the time I felt like a displaced foreigner. Curious and searching for clues I looked out across the vast non corporeal expanse. I could not comprehend. What I saw, or what I thought I saw was a symbiotic array of nonmolecular imagery. It was unfolding like the painted bridge to nowhere. Like a crazed Bohemian my mind blotted out; Off in the distance painted ponies were flying like equestrian Seraphim. These angel- winged guardians were protecting non existential thrones adorned with astrological signs of milky way heritage. The zodiac seats of privilege were draped in waterfall constellations. They were scattered about in a lofty haze between exotic rings of garland and a sparkling crop circle maze. In the spatial hierarchy pentagrams were twinkling. They looked to be ancient hieroglyphs connected to Orion's belt. Or melodic holograms revolving in the sinuous mist of séance invocation. Looking to the heavens I had a revelation. I realized that for at least a day the soothing breath of Vishnu was the primary substance supporting this spectral whirlwind. From the climate of eminence a cat's cradle of shooting stars took flight. Pinwheels unraveling left trails of tinsel. Cosmic strings absorbed strands of twilight. Towering nebulae were expanding like kaleidoscopic funnels. Ionized carousels collapsed into ultraviolet tunnels. The silhouette of an enlightened chorus could be seen through veils of Christmas solitude. These joyful beacons were non reflective in ribbon bow stratus. Across mystic skies fluorescent kites were sailing. Rainbow gardens flourishing. Acrobatic flocks of Loons graceful and free. A bustling forest of sunflower discs ebbed and glowed.

A gaseous eclipse was dripping like candy cane crimson. A soaring ensemble of flowering imprints crisscrossed the fairy tale foliage masking non terrestrial pigments below.

    It was somewhere between here and there that a paranormal ripple altered the vague undefined horizon. A shape-shifting hemisphere transformed into a billowing solstice plateau. Its undulating demeanor took me back to the adolescence of lava lamp overtures. Back in the altitude of black light densities I soon regressed to the caves of neanderthals. After fifty thousand dreams I finally realized that their primordial essence blended with the elliptical contour of coral indigenous pastures. In close proximity metallic fountains were ablaze. A courtyard dalliance in the palace of Zeus. Wind swept creation aligned with the mecca of no more sorrow. Radiant prisms were melting. Solar reflections glistening. Blossoming ornaments swirled. Emerald pyramids were floating like a synchronous ballet. Pearl white canopies swayed like an amorphic bouquet. Spiraling auras danced as if they were divine entities resurrected in northern light paradise. This breathtaking atmosphere was an astonishing poetic elixir. I felt like Peter Pan fluttering in a clear atrium at sunrise.

    In spite of these incredible novelties, still mesmerized by the harmonic pageantry, in the midst of this visual ambrosia I became startled. A queer feeling of uneasiness crossed my brow. My alter ego stuttered. Not yet on the brink of paranoia. Thinking that something was just not right. With the angst of a medieval alchemist on the cusp of danger, I was compelled to look back. Through low lying fog I caught a fleeting glimpse of a weary procession. A woeful assortment of ghost-like menagerie. They appeared to be roaming aimlessly through an empty passage. Blank expressions reflecting barren fields. Their gleaming footprints crystallized. The cryptic non geometric impressions were quietly forming a lustrous incandescent mesh. As one would expect, these unbelievable fluctuations of reality skewed my senses. I began to languish. My concentration wavered. My identity and purpose came into doubt. This immaculate conceptualization was becoming precarious. While engaged in this enigmatic contemplative I was suddenly jetted into the zone of oracles. I foresaw the storm of dread approaching. The vanguard to the grim reaper was cast in dusk. Swiftly it neutralized this idyllic looking glass parsel. This unparalleled parallel universe inherent to the Fellowship of the Zone. My attitude and clarity flickered. Suspicious incantations illuminated. Like a celestial avalanche, mirrored shadows of astronomical intensity befell this quixotic sanctuary of bliss.

Despite internal warning signals. Defiantly ignoring reason and creeping paranoia. After taking a brief moment to calm exacerbated survival instincts, I continued to tightrope the fragile whimsical element. As expected each step was a calculated risk riddled with doubt. However, like snowfall upon the meadow of serenity, serendipity dared. Deep breathing became dominant. This metaphysical interlude in the wake of sighs slowed tachycardia. My labile amplitude of self-confidence steadied. With ego robust an occult-rhythm arose with palpable arterial cadence. Each spellbinding pulse mystical with transcendence. A sense of amazement flared. Regretfully my time in this state of elevated perception was short lived. Like a firefly vanishing in darkness this captivating sorcery was channeled. Like Pandora's pestilence an apocalyptic nightmare began it's slithering crawl. Ruin and lost regions of vacuity spread like pathogens. Predatory tremors shook the frozen tundra. Ominous dispositions glared. Insatiable eyes rotated in vaporous isolation. The hypothermic plexus loomed with voracious intent. Darkened clouds bellowed. Avian scavengers were circling the rigid textures of this wasteland metamorphosis. I noticed only briefly the icy sheath shifting. Like deadly tentacles, watery seepage began oozing through propagating sharp tooth cracks. During the devastation my frostline peninsula shattered. I became adrift in this Purgatorial habitat. I was stranded on a rogue sheet of frosty micro dot. Floating in peril between craters of blackness

I watched menacing slabs of ice collide. Glacial crevasses threatened the arctic swell. Then swish boom-splash, a here then gone life changing spell. Into the Poseidon dimension through sharp as glass spindles I fell. Like a conspicuous intruder I was stupefied in this turbulent polar calamity. Being submerged in this pre mammalian nether world was like being siphoned into the lurking plasma of schizophrenic distortion. Through the eyes of impact and terror I saw nothing but chaotic bubbles and oscillating aqueous vectors. They looked like occult filaments zig zagging in wild ritualistic patterns. Primal aggression ruled. The sobering thought that I was no more than a nutritional alternative in this violent world of aquatic natural selection became a saturated hindrance. It depleted my will.

Immediately following that dismal thought, in the fallout of REM sleep detonation I found myself exiled in the explosive state of intractable panic. It was like being dropped into the numbing reality of unforgiving warfare. I was totally immersed. Paralysis ensued like suspended animation. My analogy being that it was as if I was a soulful dissident struggling in Neptune's sacred pool of primordial nectar. Or a crucified apostle symbolically abandoned in the dark matter between expanding galaxies. But then a miraculous advent. I was abruptly propelled into the psychological womb of fetal tranquility. Touched by amniotic warmth my body ascended. My terrified mind was freed by the distant sound of a soft motherly voice. But all too soon this shelter of uterine perfection transformed. Once again I found myself in the terrifying grasp of life-threatening frenzy. I was thrashing with savage gyrations like those of exorcism. Like a seizing epileptic mistakenly injected with a fiery bolus of adrenaline. Frantically I was fighting against the freezing unrelenting current.

    Looking up I could see the jagged hole that swallowed me whole. Sunlight filled the broken ice field like a shining star vision. Rays of light were pouring into the nautical dungeon like photonic rain. They diverged and refracted. Like a seismic blur deeper they passed into the cold liquid darkness. Becoming dimmer and dimmer. Disappearing like exo-planet radio waves into the abysmal unknown. I began graveling. I remember fighting. Kicking with faint resistance. My torso was flailing. My arms reaching in manic desperation for the jagged light source above. The current so cold continued pushing me harder and farther. My last breath grew short. How a peyote shaman's rite of passage summons the realm of Mescalito(1). Like in the psychotic abyss. Cerebral dream hypoxia invoked hallucination. In slow psychedelic motion the translucent rays of light entwined. A glowing network of lifesaving ropes was being woven. An underwater refuge gracefully evolved.

Like the long winding tales of Middle Earth, magical ladders of an Arcadian monastic harbor suddenly appeared. They were beautifully choreographed illusions. Similar to those described by lone sailors at sea whilst fighting Poseidon's wrathful surge. Like a frenetic madman I grabbed for them. Each time I had one in hand I triumphantly rejoiced. Each time promising everlasting devotion. Forever a dedicated servant. Forever glorifying the revered cult of spirituality. But the alluring "ropes of compassion" (2) were but a mirage in the deep. My fear escalated beyond words. In a flood of hysteria I became ensnared by an inexorable deluge. I became unhinged by Darwinian-Religious rapture; I must survive, I cannot die, I will not die, I am too strong to die. Oh my god! Oh no what is happening? Oh no, I think I might die? Oh my God, Oh My God I am going to die! God help me please please don't let me die. Not here, not now. Please someone save me! The current was getting colder and stronger. I was slowly being pushed farther and farther away from the fading jagged white light. Then, like a saving grace, with the force of a sonic boom, from the nuclear undercurrent hyper cognizance erupted. I could feel the adrenaline rush beginning to wear off. My distraught vasculature dilating. I knew I had to make one last all-out effort for survival. The cold and the fear diverted. With the ferocious resolve of a starving carnivore I gathered every ounce of energy that I had left. I felt invincible. I focused my entire being toward the shrinking life-saving portal above. I was acutely aware that precious milliseconds were passing. I could sense that the time was right. Replete with the intrepid conviction of an immortal soul. Arisen reptilian instincts from our phylogenetic reservoir. Bereft of cause, I became consumed by primitive blood thirsty zest. It was from this kingdom of ego that I made my final single pointed lunge.

The icy current was so strong, so fast, so cold. Desperation returned! I could not reach the ropes of compassion or the jagged edges of light, of life. I became the manifestation of pure terror. Confusion exploded. Feelings of helplessness engulfed my fledgling existence. I was inundated without hope. At that point I knew all hope was lost. I was trapped in an intermediate state frozen somewhere in time. An unwilling participant in the Davy Jones medley of horror. Lost in space. I still shiver when I recall that moment. Even though I know the suffering was not real.

It was the next dream event that blew open new horizons. It was like two completely different dreams had occurred, but not. All of a sudden, I found myself way up in a clear light sky looking down at the indignant icy river below. Sun was shining through transparent clouds and the wintry landscape blushed with blue-white sensitivity.

Everything was quiet and peaceful. It was as if I was standing on a mountain top overlooking the Great Divide with no sense of direction. Like being surrounded by a calm peaceful aura. Free from anxiety and fear. Not agitated or excited about up-coming events. It felt as if I was one and the same with all that I saw. There were no emotional responses. My random states of neurosis and O.C.D. were inactive. It was as if they were played out residues from past life karma spanning millennia. That frame of indifference was a beautiful clear light. Nothing more. I can honestly say yes, this incredible moment was Utopic.

After an unknown amount of time, if time exists in that unimaginable realm, I looked down at the river again. I noticed a small dark object rushing in a streaking silver wave. I assumed it was a disconnected log but somehow it seemed different. During this moment of what can best be described as aerial perplexity, my perch in Shangri-La quivered. Discomfort and queasiness initiated their gastric drain. My wavering feeling of serenity became overwrought. I was magnetically drawn to the morbid oddity below. I could not resist its mystique. Like Odysseus under the spell of Homer's bewitching Sirens of doom, I was succumbing to its song of peril. Then BOOM! In less than a blink of an eye I was jolted from the beautiful sky-light oasis. I found myself hovering an arms length above dire straits watching the odd shaped log being carried away by destiny. From that vantage, after a closer look I could see that what seemed to be a log was not a log at all. While struggling in the confounding stranglehold of bewilderment and consternation, I saw that this log was in dream reality a lifeless male human body. Being in the midst of this most unusual predicament, to say the least, my dispirited temptation to examine this weird omen grew into an unrelenting hypnotic chant.

    Without choice I reluctantly pursued this, what I thought could be a nefarious revelation. Through the hesitant eyes of caution what I witnessed was like a scene out of the Walking Dead; What I witnessed was a bloated corpse storming through blusterous solvent entombed by gray mist desolation. Maliciously wrapped in pasty clumps of shredded denim. Torn pieces of flannel oozing with blood and murky sediment clung to the battered torso like camouflage. It's bludgeoned arms were lacerated. It's hands were twisted in grotesque proportion. It's tortuous posture was veiled by the eternal shroud of remorse. The mottled caricature conformed to the cloak and dagger rapids like an old soggy ragdoll. Up, down, banging into rocks. Bouncing back and forth off the frozen shoreline. Even in the dream I remember thinking, wow, who is that poor man? What could have happened? Then zap! Back up in the vacuous sphere. From the unexplainable elevation I was once again overlooking the magical magnificent landscape and the flowing small dark dead male human form. This was where (or when) I awoke.

Tingling with effervescence I sat up in bed. I was dumb founded, amazed, and confused. After forever my discombobulation burst into the zone of smart drug awareness. Embracing this unbridled energy I began to think; What was that all about? Who was that dead guy floating down the river? What could have happened? Why did I have this crazy dream? There must be a rational reason. I sat there for a long time trying to figure it all out. I could not come up with rhyme or reason; Maybe it was a manifestation of pent-up emotion? Maybe it was the food I ate. Maybe it was a premonition-hopefully not. Maybe it was nothing? But whatever it was or was not I would be stricken by it's intrusive hum for many years to come.(Note; The above was an attempt to give a glimpse into an experience that occurred while uninhibited in the melodramatic chamber of sleep. It is interesting to note that Freud considered these translucent states of consciousness to be the most personal and intimate moments of human experience. Freud also considered these occasions arisen from the unshackled subconscious, these phenomena called dreams to be "the guardians of sleep"(3).)

As stated, during a fateful meditation session many

years ago this Fantasia emerged from the haunted chasm of memory like an intrusive mythological phantom. It appeared suddenly like a stray black cat peering through the window of cognition. But unlike the myriad of thoughts and memories that arise and are allowed to drift into the emptiness of inherent existence during meditation, I decided to use this unresolved interface as my contemplative focus. It was while a visitor in this vista of zone that the essence, or in terms of Buddhist philosophy, the totality of the dream finally came to light.

As explained, in the dream I was in an inescapable death struggle. I was exhausted, horrified, frightened beyond insanity. During the most frightful scene in the dream I was thinking, "This is it I am going to die. God help me please, please someone save me!". I was in terminal distress, suffocating in the plight of consummate fear. Then out of nowhere, in the blink of an eye I found myself in a beautiful, safe and peaceful environment. This acute change in settings was like a strange oxymoron. Yet during the dream this aberrant transition seemed like a normal event. It didn't seem like I was anywhere I should not be or that anything eccentric had happened. It wasn't until after I awoke that I thought it to be a fantastic yet unsettling mind-blowing experience.

This dream motivated me to research dreams and near-death experiences. I began talking with others who have had bad dreams and nightmares. I read various articles and books about near death experiences and about having what can be called-death dreams. During my informal research I came across a theory put forth by many, including some psychologists(4), that suggests that people cannot see themselves die in their own dreams. This theory states that because of the unmitigated fear that we experience during these bad dreams we wake up before the tragedy completes its course. Another theory suggests that during the life-or-death struggle fear is created in the struggling dream body's consciousness. This energy that we call fear then travels through a subconscious conduit into the dreamer's autonomic nervous system. This ghastly impulse then triggers the fight or flight response. This response then cultivates fear in other parts of the dreamer's sleep consciousness. It is the accumulation of fear in these other areas that causes us to wake up in fear. It has been postulated that while in the dream state several intermediate mental factors are also active(3*). Succinctly, the intermediate "dream watching" (DWC) and/or non dreaming sleep consciousnesses(NDSC). They are always present and are either aware or capable of becoming aware. There are two basic mechanisms from which fear can arise in these sleep/dream intermediate states. One is the subjective objective "dream watching" of the dream body's death struggle. The other is when the struggling dream body's consciousness is the subjective manifestation of the dreamer. When the dream body's consciousness experiences fear during the life-or-death struggle, the fight or flight centers are stimulated. Just like in the waking state. These survival centers then send panic signals into the intermediate sleep consciousness (DWC/NDSC). This panic causes fear to be created in these intermediate areas. When this fear becomes overwhelming, we inevitably wake up in fear. These explanations seemed logical but did not explain the extraordinary events that transpired in my dream.(Note; these are very streamlined explanations of the very complicated and not fully understood dream processes)

Contrary to these conventional thoughts and theories, based on my personal experience and research into so called alternative beliefs and cognitive sleep psychology(4) it is now my belief that it is possible to see ourselves die in dreams. To explain, as suggested it is the emotion of fear that wakes us up from these nightmares. Therefore, it is plausible to think that if we did not get so scared or if somehow we could overcome, transcend, or transform the energy of fear during the dream, we would not wake up from the fight or flight response.

Not being awoken by this fear generated by the fear

of death at the time of our death in the dream/nightmare, the dream would continue which would then set the stage for us to see or experience the next phase of the dream. Which could be our death or maybe something more mind boggling. Again, it is fear that wakes us up from these nightmares. If it were possible to overcome or transform this fear during any phase of the dream, we would not wake-up. If we did not wake up the potential exists that the dream would continue which would allow us to see/experience not only our death but also what happens after we die in the dream. In agreement with others who support this potential I can say with confidence that if one does see oneself die in one's own dream, one has not necessarily died in real life. Whether a dream like this is a premonition or not is another matter. These dreams of death could also have many other psychological interpretations and meanings(4).

My analysis and interpretation of this amazing non-psychotropic non- orgasmic(unfortunately) mind experience; The first realization that I had during the profound meditation session was that unlike what normally happens when one has this type of nightmare, I DID NOT WAKE UP DURING MY DEATH STRUGGLE. I believe this occurred because of my limited knowledge and practice of Tibetan Buddhism. I believe that because I have internalized some of these beliefs my dream body's consciousness, in this dream, was able to transcend or transform the emotion of fear during my dream body's life or death struggle. Because my dream body's consciousness overcame fear during my(1') life or death struggle, the fight or flight center was not aroused and therefore did not send panic signals into the DWC/NDSC. Because panic signals were not sent to the DWC/NDSC, fear was not created. Because fear was not created in these areas I did not wake up in fear. I did not wake up.

Because my struggling dream body's consciousness miraculously overcame fear, instead of waking up in fear my dream body's consciousness, spirit, soul, whatever left my struggling near-death dream body. It transcended into a blissful after-death dream panorama. "I" suddenly found myself hovering untethered to flesh and blood soma. (This dream was similar to those who have had "real life" near- death experiences.) Furthermore, while in this after-death dream stratus "I"(the dream body's consciousness transcended) was able to look below and see a corpse floating down icy **River Death.** This was a stunning realization for me. But the next realization was even more shocking. It was psychological suffocation fueled by fumes of anarchy. It was like being surrounded by an army of screaming blood thirsty Banshees in the night. It is still hard for me to express sometimes. But what it was, what I realized while in this profound meditative state was that the poor dead man who was helplessly flowing down River Death-WAS ME! It was me! It was my body floating down the icy River Death! I was immediately jolted from meditative equipoise. Abruptly I transitioned into my "normal" neurotic condition, but even more so. Arising from this meditation session was like waking from a nightmare. After gathering myself I remember thinking, that's it! Instead of waking up in fear when my dream body was about to die, my dream consciousness, spirit, soul, whatever transcended my dying dream body. "I" transcended into the dreams (or maybe it was the "real") Akashic Plane(5). And what was even more ridiculous was that I realized that the poor male corpse that "I" saw floating down River Death was mine! I thought holy shit, that's it! It was I who had died, drowned in the river. What actually happened was that I fell through the ice into the river. I was drowning. Sometime during the death struggle the energy from the fear of death was transformed into a cool calm dream consciousness. Because of this sub psychologic anomaly the fight or flight response was not triggered and therefore panic and fear were not created in the DWC/sleep consciousness. It was this change in the dream's lucidity that prevented me from being awoken in fear by fear. During or shortly after that transformation of energy "I" left my struggling near death dream body. "I" transcended into an after death realm in the dream where "I", not knowing it at the time, was able to look down and watch my dream corpse floating down the same icy dream river that I' had drowned in. I was watching my own corpse floating down River Death. WOW! What an epiphany. But that was it. This is what happened and that was what the dream was about!

This realization opened the floodgates. It just blew me away. My cognitive pathways were permanently rearranged. I was actually looking at my own corpse drifting down the icy coffin river. I could not get over it. It seemed so crazy, so far out. I then thought, could this really be it? But as time went by, the more I thought about it the more this interpretation seemed plausible. All the pieces seemed to fit. To further reinforce that this interpretation was correct was that shortly after this moment of realization the perplexing curiosity that I had for all those years subsided. The subtle sense of fear and anxiety that arose when thinking about this intrusive dream disappeared. What did remain and still remains to this day and not only when thinking about the dream, is a deep sense or feeling of calmness and serenity. It just feels right! This has to be the right interpretation. Furthermore, after much thought and reflection I believe that I developed this sense of serenity not only because I finally came to understand what the crazy dream was all about but to more significance, I acquired a unique hopeful feeling and/or insight into the death experience. Since this profound moment I have much less anxiety, confusion and fear when thinking about death, even my own. The realization strengthened my inclination *or* "sixth sense" about there being life *a*fter so called death and the possibility that other types of beings and realms really do exist. These concepts are taught by Buddhism and are currently being investigated by theoretical/quantum physics(6). This dream realization motivated me to continue the study of Buddhism and to keep up on current scientific literature.

Of all the interesting and profound thoughts precipitated from this adventure, the one I feel is most relevant in view of the pursuit of social equality and world peace is how important it is, how vital it is to learn about or to at least try to understand other ideologies and religions. For instance, based on my limited knowledge I now firmly believe that The Ancient Alien Theorists, Buddhism, Christianity, Hinduism, Islam, Judaism, many other religions/philosophies, and science all allude to this type of paranormal experience as well as the existence of some type of heavenly, euphoric, enlightened, or non-earthly dimension. Just recently theoretical physics has developed a "new" theory suggesting that "death may be an illusion and consciousness may continue after biological death"(7)(Exactly what Buddhism has explicitly taught for *2500* years). Also, the University of Virginia and other universities are doing research on reincarnation. Not to mention that Christian biblical and non-biblical gospels(Gnostic/Dead Sea Scrolls) talk in unequivocal terms, as well as in parables, about "not having to enter *a* body again"(8), after death. Based on my informal comparatives it seems that all these disciplines are talking about the same thing. After much thought I have concluded that the ingrained variability between all higher philosophical tenets and religious ideologies are merely contextual perspectives or cultural interpretations. I now believe that the foundation of all euphoric experience created during paranormal, psychotic and/or religious/spiritual practice is the same. It can be said in many ways but simply put; The origin of all religious/spiritual etc. experience lies within the brilliant infinity that I call The Amorphic Zone. These states of consciousness arise when "other" areas of the brain become activated from internal or external stimuli. An investigation into the neurophysiology and the ultimate nature of this zone are well beyond the purpose and scope of this narrative.

To me this dream was analogous and it's essence identical to explanations of near-death experiences. These severely injured people claim to have watched themselves being worked on or operated on from "above". And to cases where people who were pronounced dead miraculously came back to life after seeing an angel or the "bright white light". These experiences are universal. Documented occurrences can be found throughout history. They seem to span beyond the relative concept of time itself. These paranormal effects are ubiquitous human mind conditions that all humans (living now, in the past and most likely in the future-depending on the development of A.I.?) can relate to in one way or another. For many, these experiences are no more than esoteric sojourns into repressed zones of triviality. But to me they are important and realistic. Many of the world's greatest geniuses such as Einstein, Jobs, Tesla etc. stated that many of their world changing ideas came from "somewhere else" while they were in a dream-like or deep meditative-like trance. I believe if taken seriously these moments in the plane of unfamiliar frequencies can have a positive impact concerning one's outlook and quality of life. Whether achieved through psychotropics, prayer, meditation, exhaustion, orgasm etc. this "Journey To The Center Of The Mind"(9), or Zone, or Heaven or a higher level of consciousness, whatever you want to call it indicate that there is a uniform matrix *and/or* a universal consciousness, or realm, or non-all creator God state that we belong to or are intrinsically connected with. I believe it is an awakened environment that we have access to while alive and well or not well. While awake or asleep.

In this age of quantum technology, it is fairly easy to find information from which one can integrate and synthesize dynamic interrelationships and identify incontrovertible parallels between science and religion. Based on my informal analytic investigation and personal experience I now believe that these extraordinary endowments and experiences of mind, these overlapping quantum planes of consciousness are valid and that all people(and others) possess the potential to increase their awareness and therefore their appreciation of them. I believe that it is possible for all people to develop a greater understanding of this universal, non-fictional vibrant zone. It has been said, "It is not unique for us to be unique; it is unique for us to understand and embrace our universal non- uniqueness".

To the non-atheist, River Death can be thought of as a conduit connecting the relative mundane to the ultimate other. To the atheist, River Death leads one to the end of struggle and suffering.

In conclusion I will share one more of my realizations from this experience with you. This little realization was nothing more than an acute insight into the essence of a particular common-sense reality that to me is neither good nor bad. This collective reality is; Regardless of how many people work to develop their universal compassionate potential, if and only if all people endeavor to obtain this enlightened state can world peace be achieved and sustained. The only way world peace is possible is if we, all members of this Earthly community embrace the Amorphic Zone and strive to abide in the harmonious condition of cognitive unity. To initiate this seemingly formidable task one must first analytically evaluate and compare the various belief systems and theories that subscribe to the occurrence of these alternative mental or spiritual experiences. Through thoughtful analysis and logical deduction one can then piece together a complex yet simplistic psychological puzzle. As stated above, information concerning these notions is readily available. Whether one wishes to call them alternative, paranormal, holy/spiritual etc. does not matter. It has become clear to me that regardless of the impetus all these mind experiences originate from the same source. All these phenomena result from altered neuro physiology and are merely illuminated pathways that lead to or from the ultimate matrix, the Amorphic Zone. I truly believe it would be a great benefit if one were to increase one's understanding of these alternative/extra sensory experiences. Not only on a personal level but to society and to the world. I sincerely believe that if all people were to embrace this "Fellowship of the Zone" a more compassionate, understanding, and profound new world order would arise.

Maybe someday, maybe some place, maybe some time. It is there somewhere for all of us. And it begins, with me.

SOME REFERENCES

(For a realistic list of references, one must not only cite innumerable known texts of literature, philosophy, religion, science, psychology and their sub genres, but also the comprehensive works once located in the Great Library of Alexandria. As well as other lost or unknown books containing ancient/contemporary knowledge).

1 - A Separate Reality; Carlos Castaneda

2 -Tibetan Book Of The Dead; The Bardo of Becoming; Author unknown. Karma Lingpa. Padmasambhava. Choyam Trungpa. Wisdom Publication.

I - Denotes my normal waking consciousness.
I' - Denotes my dream body and dream body's consciousness connected "I"- Denotes:
> 1. Strictly my dream body's consciousness
> 2. My transcended dream consciousness separated from my dream body
> 3. My inert, intermediate dream watching/ sleep consciousness.

3 - Sleeping, Dreaming and Dying: The Dalai Lama and Francisco J. Varela, Ph.D Wisdom Publications.

3*- Contemporary Psychology and Buddhist Dream yoga teach that there is often more than one state of consciousness/subconsciousness active while sleeping and dreaming. In general, they postulate that active or inactive mental states exist simultaneously between the manifest dream and the edge of wakefulness. These intermediate or inert sleep states may or may not be aware that there is dreaming. These sleep states in some way are connected with the fight or flight autonomic nervous system. When fear arises in the dream it triggers the fight or flight response which then triggers or stimulates fear to arise in these intermediate sleep states. It is postulated that this double fear (present simultaneously in the manifest dream and in the intermediate sleep state) becomes so overwhelming that it generates the geyser of fear that causes us to wake up in the cold sweat of fear.(This is a very general and simplistic description of one theory concerning the dream/sleep process. Much research has been done and is currently being done in the cognitive/subconscious/dream sleep disciplines. There is still much to learn.)

4.- Psychology Today; "What Dreams of Your Death Are Really About." Seth J. Gillihan PhD. Feb.2016.

5.- Wisdom of the Ancients: Some Eastern Religious traditions would explain this experience as an astral projection into the astral plane in which one's silver cord is severed. These traditions believe that this is what happens when one dies in "real life". They claim the astral plane is also accessible in dreams and during meditation. The point being in view of this narrative, is that we can enter the astral plane when we die, when we dream and when we die in our dreams; Lobsang Rampa. 1965. Dasherbooks.

6 - Nautilus Science Magazine; Issue 47; Robert Pentrose on Why Consciousness Does Not Compute: Steve Paulson.

7 - Newsweek; Tech and Science: Where do you go when you die? The Increasing Signs that Human Consciousness Remains after Death; Kastalia Medrano 2/10/18.

7* - Psychology Today: Is Death an Illusion, Evidence Suggests Death isn't the End; Robert Lanza M.D. Nov 11, 2011

8 - The Secret Book of John; The Apocryphon of John, Six Questions about the Soul.

8* - Reincarnation in the Bible: Keven Williams; B.Sc.

9   -The Amboy Dukes, "Journey To The Center Of The Mind." *Journey to the Center of the Mind.* Mainstream Records. 1968. Album.

Observed Dream Movement: Zone

ARCTIC HUNGER

Clinging to rainbow dreams
Frost line colors blinding white
Refractory within psychotic abyss-

Invocation of desolate forms and distant phantoms from vacuity
Monstrous ravaging anger unleashed-
Cavernous winds, swirling mountainous squall,
Subliminal tundra mani
Arctic hunger insatiable

Weary infant devoured.

J. Munro Jr.

A WINTER'S NIGHTMARE

If you fall through ice into the river unclean
If you fall through this fragile facade of beauty,
    Where wrathful deities cannibalize when fed
Where with voracious eyes stir their vile cauldron mesh
Where invertebrate slavers through blood horizons sail
Where skulls beaten into sacculus of flesh
Where rabid memories regress to neanderthal
Where open sore macabre savage
Where your face is grotesque like sharp tooth eel
Where this icy tomb a sea monster's net
Where abruptly awoken from deep sleep trolling
A winter's nightmare you will not forget.

Observed Dream Movement: Zone

MELTING PRISM

Like mammoth mausoleum melting
Bedrock caverns emit hallucination
Prisms unobstructed drench grassland hue
Bones preserved in toothless mound
           Siberian snow a carnivore

Remote,
        Vanishing,
Black mold timber chromatic
Carcasses pose in glint
Terracotta apparitions glazed by skyline thaw
Epiphanies resemble OM horizon,

Abstract pigments anoint fields of silt
Emerald foliage sparkling like tiara
Diamond necklace flora
Arcadian hilltop aura
Silk Road sun wheel ambiance
Cerebral spectrum a far-reaching canvas,

Rainbow from the pure Heart-
Tree line mantra.

J. Munro Jr.

RIVER INSANITY

Rapid silver ceiling deafening
Acoustic asylum
Bubbling graffiti disturbs aquatic parasites
Cynical bottom feeders absorb schio-hierarchy
Omniscience constricts,
River of Orphans turbulent,

With trepidation willows weeping do ebb
Idiosyncrasies swallow maniacal sneer
Contorted swarm core sarcastic
Archaic dementia fragile
Flouting sediment degrades moronic undertow,

Quagmire therapy satirical
Aesthetically distraught like currents moving corpses,
Absurd paradox-whirlpool of depression
        Amphibious odyssey bipolar
Mouth of insanity open.

Observed Dream Movement: Zone

INDIGENOUS RAPTURE

My essence now River Death
Forest ashen strange agonal breath
Fearful this moment O' mortal dread
Trees petrified hanging vultures dead
Wolves hunt screeching Reapers thrive
Haunting sallow habit
Grim nomadic tribe,

Anemic pulse, gangrene then carnage
Sheaths of humanity silent in starvation
My body will nourish roots of flowers
Mother Nature is pleased
Non-amniotic voyage a saga through tranquility
Shroud of life unveiled
Indigenous rapture.

J. Munro Jr.

AFTER THE APOCALYPSE

My essence now perfectly gray
Frameless then distant shores erupt
Self cherishing empire of ego betrayed
Synaptic relics tarnished
Quantum seizures abrupt,

Amorphic landscape contradicts knowledge
Waning intellect forgotten
Ice-age monoliths reflect luminous isolation
Untamed refuge
Inner monastery
Surreal wasteland ripens
        Atrophied

Rouge pastels
Bleak sticks
Uprooted desire
Exhaustion
Despair
Duality within orgasm-nowhere,

Observed Dream Movement: Zone

Ego existence extinct Non-existent fallou

Emptiness evolves from delusionary panic-

Apocalyptic survival.

J. Munro Jr.

ASYSTOLIC JOURNEY

Released, pernicious endothelial abscess gutted
Loneliness filling gastric cesspool drain
Deep fear contemplating fear nonexistent
Peristaltic emotions waveless
Interlude   In vein
Time a pulseless strait
Fathomless heartless wait,
Asystolic journey
                Asystolic journey ascending canyon
Void,

Weightlessly soaring in the eye of hurricanes
Looking below at first dawn unrecognized
Reality meaningless
Cascading poetry
Non reflective free fall into the grave of angelic dusk,

Reasoning beyond reason-soaring beyond
Beginningless whispering mantra heard
Celestial bouquet of primordial eons
Amplified waterfalls cradling echo,

Observed Dream Movement: Zone

Oceans pass
Centuries revolve without anger
Breathlessly silent
Beholding non-judgment
Watching with no pain from eagle's domain-

My corpse without fear

My corpse in the river below.

J. Munro Jr.

PRE-HISTORIC FLIGHT

Beginningless   zone   parabolic   vacuum
    Harmonic velvet in white   Eagle's
    Domain   sovereign   transcendent
    Immaculate Conception   Circular
    In flight,

Peaceful deities cross peerless stream
Primordial vortex ventilates aboriginal site
In prehistoric coffin to ocean extreme
To transcendent cradle where eagles
Fly
From deathless timeless godless chariot
Soaring I watched in wonder;
My corpse floating like a still born vestige
Like an aborted fetus born free Celebrating-
Not infected by Trump voter's fraudulent religion,

      Entities   Flying

             Exist
                   One root

Observed Dream Movement: Zone

    Spacious

          House with no more sorrow

    Native echo
          Directionless

Reincarnation..

ABOUT THE AUTHOR

Mom was a devout Catholic. Dad was a devout Darwinian Atheist. And I, stuck in the middle, I just wanted the attention and love from both of them. In retrospect, I believe it was in large part my simultaneous exposure to those polarized beliefs that resulted in my muddled state of self consciousness and unsettling neurosis. I developed a personality that was obsessed with trying to understand everything yet unable to distinguish clear boundaries between fantasy and reality. Between here and the hereafter. Between Angels and flying monkeys. As a child I thought that Angels and flying monkeys were somehow related! Because of my innate and acquired psychological profile I spent much time trying to balance and equate the esoteric theology of Christianity with science, logic and other theoretical principles. At some point during my education, evolution, my search for the truth if you will, I came across the teachings of the one called Buddha. These teachings somehow made sense to me. For me these teachings added a whole new dimension to the indoctrinated matrix that I was exposed to. I was finally able to paint a different, somewhat more integrated picture of life, death, after-death and my relationship with them. I have been an adherent to Tibetan Buddhism ever since.

I work as a respiratory therapist in a hospital outside of Detroit. I have been very fortunate not to have contracted Covid-yet. Unfortunately many of my peers, associates and especially EMS personnel were not so lucky. Especially during the onset of the virus onslaught when no one knew what was going on. If Trump did not lie about Covid being fake, if he was more concerned about helping us, and our country, rather than protecting his own personal agenda he could have chosen to better equip and prepare us for the battle. If Trump did not lie, if he told the truth about Covid maybe he could have helped us! I worked on several EMS personnel and nurses that died early on-when Covid was fake! Had he done that, had he chosen to be a hero rather than the fake that he is he would still be president. He would have become a great president. Even greater than the one that he thinks he was.

Concerning politics - I consider myself to be an independent. Although I find very few principles attached to the republican agenda that I agree with. Case in point, abortion. I do not feel one bit bad for the unborn. They will never experience the confusion, struggles or suffering inherent to this life, to this world. If nothing else these unborn will be safe in the warm house of God. Why do the Repubs think that it is so important that these unwanted children be born? Why do they ignore God's gift of free will? I have been taught that if God wants a person to be born, God will make sure that that person is born! Is it that the Repubs lack faith or maybe have no faith or belief in God at all? (They do believe or support the 20,000 lies of their politicians) The decision of birth is an intimate, sacred moment between God and mother. That unique connection should be cherished and respected by everyone. It is no one's right to interfere with this holy bond between God and potential mother. I do believe it is righteous to try to influence an impregnated women to have the child.

But to take away her choice is violating God's gift of free will. Forced birth is also a violation of human/women's rights. Obstructing women's choice with fear and force is perverting her relationship with God. Meddling with this relationship between God and women during this most beautiful and sacred time is both a violation of women's rights and a sacrilege. The Bible supports this. "He that is without sin among you, let him first cast a stone at her".

Birth is a decision that is to be made EXCLUSIVELY through the holy communion between God and women. Not by man made law created by imperfect politicians and religious zealots who have trouble keeping their own houses in order! Not only do Republicans lack the qualifications to override God's gift of free will, they absolutely lack the knowledge and qualifications to tell a woman what to do with her body, how to run her life! Birth is a personal event that should be brought forth in unobstructed love-Blessed by God. The decision to have an abortion (before the fetus is capable of surviving on its own, independent of the womb) is not a political football. It is an inexpressible moment of intimacy between God and women. Trust them! Trust God's gift of choice!

www.ingramcontent.com/pod-product-compliance
Lightning Source LLC
LaVergne TN
LVHW011832060526
838200LV00053B/3982